Langer
on Putting

Langer on Putting

Bernhard Langer
with Vivien Saunders

Illustrations by Chris Perfect

Stanley Paul
London Melbourne Auckland Johannesburg

Stanley Paul & Co. Ltd

An imprint of Century Hutchinson Ltd,

62–65 Chandos Place, London WC2N 4NW

Century Hutchinson Australia (Pty) Ltd
PO Box 496, 16–22 Church Street, Hawthorn, Melbourne,
Victoria 3122, Australia

Century Hutchinson New Zealand Limited
PO Box 40–086, Glenfield, Auckland 10, New Zealand

Century Hutchinson South Africa (Pty) Ltd
PO Box 337, Bergvlei 2012, South Africa

First published 1987
© Bernhard Langer 1987
Illustrations © Chris Perfect 1987

Set in Monophoto Century

Printed and bound in Great Britain
by Butler & Tanner Ltd, Frome and London

British Library Cataloguing in Publication Data

Langer, Bernhard
   Langer on putting.
   1. Putting (Golf)
   I. Title   II. Saunders, Vivien
   796.352′35   GV979.P8

ISBN 0 09 164350 3

Contents

Acknowledgements

The authors and publishers would like to thank Lawrence Levy of Yours in Sport for all the specially commissioned photography, and Peter Dazeley, Lawrence Levy and Phil Sheldon for the use of their copyright photographs.

Foreword

The world's press and golfing public became fully aware of the potential brilliance of Bernhard Langer in 1979. He had been playing with some success on the European tour but, like most young professionals, was searching for that one major win which would set him on the road to stardom. His is an unusual background by professional golf standards. No German before had ever been thought of as a world-class player, and Germany, by its nationals' own admission, could only be considered as a very minor golfing nation. Then, in 1979, Bernhard Langer hit the headlines. None of the golfing press were in any doubt that a new European star had emerged. The scene was Nîmes, venue of the World Under-25 Championship. Langer started with a 73. Nothing glorious in that, leaving him amongst a pack of young men all with talent and desire and many with more illustrious pedigrees than the young German. But from the second round onwards the tournament was Langer's and Langer's alone.

His second round saw an immaculate 67, followed by another 67 on the third day and yet another on the fourth. Victory was his, not just by a whisker, not just by a shot, not just by sneaking victory over the last couple of holes, but by a devastating 17 shots. He holed everything. He peppered the flag with his iron shots, as we had seen before and were to see repeatedly again, but he also rammed in putt after putt. The putter seemed like a wand in his hand. He himself seemed bemused by the results. He visibly chuckled – not what one expects from a supposedly dour German – as a 25-foot putt he felt he had mis-struck swerved uncannily into the hole for yet another birdie. It was as though he couldn't believe it.

We had seen him struggling before to get to grips with the slick greens of Europe's championship courses. Previously he had clearly been unnerved by the transition from his slow home greens in Germany to those of Britain and the Continent. But in Nîmes he seemed to have mastered it, seemed to have put all the previous doubts and indecisions behind him, clearly becoming more confident, not just on the greens, but with his long game, as each of the seventy-two holes was virtually faultlessly completed.

And then it went again. The rest of 1979 saw poor Bernhard struggling. His long game continued to be immaculate. His iron shots were precise and his driving immensely long and accurate. But for some reason there was this niggling problem on the greens. He wasn't unsuccessful. No one who fires the ball repeatedly to within 15 feet of the flag can do anything but score well. But for Bernhard these shots produced pars and not the string of birdies which would have resulted from a putting touch matching the rest of his game. It was at times heartbreaking to see.

In 1980 Bernhard bounced back from the putting doldrums. In the March of that year he won the British Car Auctions Tournament at Sunningdale. Granted, it was a relatively minor tournament and the greens by tournament standards were relatively slow and bumpy and not so far removed from those back in Germany. It was at the same venue later in the year that Seve Ballesteros came to Bernhard's rescue. He suggested a change of putter from a rather short, light, centre-shafted Bullseye to something heavier which would swing itself, in the hope of stopping the yipping action which was beginning to worry the Langer fans. In Clive Clark's shop at Sunningdale he invested the meagre sum of £5 on a heavier, flanged version of this style of putter. Things began to improve, albeit spasmodically, and by the end of the season Langer seemed once again to be finding the touch necessary for a true champion. At the end of the year he recorded his first major win with the Dunlop Masters at St Pierre on the English–Welsh border. The greens again were not particularly fast, not those glasslike, shimmering greens which face the competitors in the world's true major championships. But he had arrived. Here he was, Dunlop Masters Champion of 1980. His penetrating iron shots, combined with putting which was only average by professional standards, had taken him clear of an illustrious European and overseas field of stars.

He was quietly confident. He now knew he could win in Europe, and we knew that he clearly had the ability to score success worldwide. There was just a doubt in the back of everyone's mind that the putting might let him down. He consolidated his position in 1981, leading the money list in Europe and impressing all who saw him. The British and European crowds warmed to his quiet, businesslike approach to the game. His style was so unlike that of the other emerging star, Ballesteros. The Spaniard was exciting by contrast. His was a game in which you never quite knew what was going to happen. He reminded the crowds of Arnold Palmer. Here was another hero who would clatter the ball into the trees, make a remarkable

recovery, and then slot in a gigantic putt with a glare or a smile, and with the sheer cheek and arrogance towards the golf course that the true amateur loves to see. But for the purists it was Langer who was emerging as the European hopeful. To some it was unthinkable that a man should win the British Open, as Ballesteros had done, having to extricate himself from a car park (albeit a special on-course car park) at Lytham St Annes. It wasn't on. Langer was different. His long game was one of real precision and sound method. It didn't leave the spectator or golf writer with heart pounding and wondering where the next shot was going. It was so exact, so mechanical and so extraordinarily predictable – until he got onto the greens.

The problem worsened through 1982. Still the drives ripped past most of his contemporaries. Still the iron shots were hammered home with relentless authority. But the putting was suspect. Peter Alliss, his own career having been dogged by bad putting, could on one or two occasions hardly contain his distress in commentating as another Langer birdie slipped away. The yips were back, and the faster the greens the more he seemed prone to lose his touch and control and, with them, the birdies. The right hand would suddenly jerk and the putter seemed to leap forward with a mind of its own, shooting the ball past the hole. It was only once or twice a round, but this was enough to keep Langer from the winner's circle. These were the days when John McEnroe was smashing his tennis racket, hurling abuse at officials and spectators, and throwing himself to the ground like a mindless idiot at the slightest sign of frustration. But Langer with perfect selfcontrol soldiered on. Inside, his heart must have been pounding, and surely he was seething with rage at his own ineptitude. But outwardly he was calm and ever cheerful, seemingly either learning to live with the problem or quietly confident that it would disappear.

The golfing spectators love the professional to make a thoroughly bad shot. In their heart of hearts they love seeing Ballesteros in the trees. They relish the thought of some poor unfortunate star coming unstuck in a watery grave at Augusta. It makes them seem human.

But what every golfer sympathizes with is the missed short putt. Rarely does it produce a horrible groan from the crowd, more an embarrassed silence. The crowd sympathized with Langer. Here was a young man so obviously talented, so clearly streets ahead of many of his contemporaries, and yet suffering what they suffered. Make no mistake about it, the results were still excellent and Langer was a constant threat. The golfing public

Opposite: A moment of anguish

wrote to him in vast numbers. Their kindness in many ways was quite extraordinary. They took time and much effort to write letters with all manner of putting tips and suggestions, things they had noticed on the television, points they had picked out from watching him in person. Manufacturers wanted him to try every kind of putter imaginable. He was offered advice from hypnotists and psychologists. Letters followed him from tournament to tournament until eventually catching up with his globe-trotting routine.

But for Langer it was a question of work: hard, relentless, untiring work and practice. Through 1981 and 1982 he had tried virtually everything, but with the constraint of having to try out any new technique in a competitive situation. It was hard to try something new in a tournament, and several theories offering more than a glimmer of hope had to wait until he could experiment with them away from the pressures of the tour. His guide and mentor from the early years, Willi Hofmann from Munich, was a tower of strength. Hofmann had undying confidence in his young protégé. He had seen him hole virtually every makable putt on the slow, bumpy greens of Germany. Between them they knew he had the skill and coordination to adjust. It was a matter of researching every possible factor in putting until they could find why the breakdown occurred, and then building a new method.

Langer had experimented with putting cross-handed. Mind you, he had experimented with virtually everything. But in October 1982 he played a series of television matches with Greg Norman at Woburn Golf Club in England. This was the time to make changes. There was a degree of pressure with the television cameras present, but it wasn't the same pressure as on the tournament circuit. He decided to putt cross-handed and to stick with it through thick and thin. It apparently felt awkward and at times he seemed uncomfortable. But it began to work. Long-putting had never been any problem for Langer; his touch was excellent. Gradually the short-putting began to take shape. By the middle of 1983 Langer looked a different man. It was still at times unnerving to see him in a state of indecision over a medium-length putt. Cross-handed or orthodox? We wished he would settle for one or the other. But surely now he was ready to win one of the major championships.

In 1984 his efforts were again concentrated on the European tour. His cross-handed putting for the shorter-range putts began to pay dividends. By the end of the year he led not only the Order of Merit but the putting statistics as well. He looked fully happy and confident with his method, with not a hint of awkwardness or indecision. Indeed, less than observant pro-am partners did not always notice anything unusual about the Langer style. He won the Open titles of Spain, Holland, Ireland and France and very nearly took the Open at St Andrews. It is sometimes said that the Americans do not take kindly to outsiders. But they took to Langer and he to them. In early 1984 he married a young American girl, Vikki, whom he had met the previous year at a tournament. With her support and companionship he was able to find the success in America which eludes so many foreigners. His eight starts in America brought him three top ten finishes and it was clear that he had the skill and tenacity to win against the world's toughest opposition. In 1985 he did just that and captured his first major championship – the US Masters at Augusta.

Ballesteros, with his victories in 1980 and 1983, had in some ways paved the way for a European success. The prospect of a German win, or indeed a non-American win, no longer sent shockwaves through the foundations at Augusta.

Before the tournament started there were those who still had their doubts about Langer's ability to win one of the majors. True, he had been knocking at the door. True, his putting problems seemed to have been overcome. But major championships provide a test that little bit more exacting. There is the added pressure, not just in prizemoney terms, but in terms of all the endorsements and business contracts which can result. For Langer it was thought that there could be an even greater demand. The greens at the major championships are often manicured and, one might think, polished to a trueness and slickness unmatched during the rest of the year. Those at Augusta are far more fearsome than the rest. To the television viewer the slopes may not be apparent. But for the player and spectator it is all too obvious that the greens at Augusta can be a potential nightmare. Tom Weiskopf, it is said, held them in such respect that he built scale models of the most punishing to familiarize himself with their intricacies. They are tricky!

Augusta at the best of times is not a course for the faint-hearted. It is long. It is tough and requires iron shots which not only hit the green but which settle in fairly specific places to leave manageable putts. Four-putting is possible. Putting off the greens is possible. Pitching on the green too short of the optimum and spinning back into the water is quite possible. And in 1985 it was even more awesome. Golf champions very rarely grumble about golf courses. No one grumbles about Augusta because such criticism simply isn't part of the tradition of the game. Register displeasure, and you might not be invited back the next year. But the greens in 1985 were so much faster than usual that two former champions, Watson and

Sharing the glory of winning with wife, Vikki

14

Nicklaus, showed some concern over their speed and the horrendous choice of two or three pin positions. But for Langer they seemed to hold no fear. Part of this was undoubtedly his extraordinarily accurate iron play and his initial positioning on the greens.

While Watson with his usual aggressive, attacking stroke three-putted at least four times in one round, Langer three-putted just once in the entire seventy-two holes. Perhaps the extraordinary speed of the greens rattled many of the world's best players more than they rattled Langer. As he acquired confidence day by day many of them seemed to lose theirs. His first two rounds were nothing out of the ordinary. Neat and tidy, leaving him well placed amongst the challengers. But on the third day with a 68, equal best of the day, he moved up into true contention.

The final day's pairing worried some of us, if not Langer himself. He was paired with Ballesteros on the same score, behind Ray Floyd and Curtis Strange. The Spaniard had always just got the better of him. Three times they had met in the final of the World Matchplay Championship. Three times the Spaniard had got his man. In the Open at St Andrews the year before they had again been paired together and again the Spaniard had edged ahead to victory. There were those who quipped that Langer didn't foresee himself winning. Who, after all, would put on scarlet trousers and matching shirt for that final round if holding any expectation of donning the winner's green jacket? But for Langer there were clearly no such doubts in his mind. This time the Spaniard's company was perhaps helpful. Far better that two Europeans should be facing the Augusta crowd together rather than suffering from partisanship when playing with one of the home heroes. Certainly Langer's concentration was unfaltering.

With six holes to go those spectators who were naive enough not to appreciate the subtleties of Augusta had assumed that victory belonged to Curtis Strange, then leading moneywinner on the tour. He was 3 ahead of Langer. Willi Hofmann was at Augusta airport ready to fly back to Germany. But it was the American who faltered in the water on the 13th and 15th and the German whose concentration and precision putting clinched victory.

The odds had been stacked against him. The toughest, fastest greens on the American tour – or, many would say, anywhere in the world – had been at their fastest and most formidable. And here was the young man from Germany, who two or three years previously looked horribly vulnerable and was at times agonizing to watch, putting his way to victory. He had proved that, with hard work, patience and belief in himself, he had

With friend and rival, Seve Ballesteros – his turn to win on that occasion

16

That Masters green jacket certainly felt good!

conquered his golfing nightmare and was a force to be reckoned with anywhere in the world.

Willi Hofmann, having heard that his student was threatening to win the title, returned breathless after a cab race across town just too late to see Langer's last putt holed for victory. But he was there to share in the glory of Langer's winning moment. There may have been an inkling of a doubt in Hofmann's mind as he had left for the airport as to whether Langer was finally cured and en route to world stardom. But by the time he arrived at the Country Club his doubts, those of the press and public and of Langer himself (if he still had any) were finally dispelled. The young man who many thought couldn't putt had not only proved that he had mastered his putting, but was the Masters Champion.

Vivien Saunders

1 My Technique

For the first ten years of my golfing life I played on slow, bumpy greens in Germany. As a youngster I was always a very good putter and by the time I became an assistant professional at Munich I was virtually infallible from 6 feet and closer. Slow, bumpy greens like the ones we had in Germany are in many ways not very demanding. If the ball doesn't go in you always feel you have an excuse because it may not have rolled very well. In many ways it was, therefore, very easy to be confident on these greens. I could blame any miss on the green and not on me. Like many golfers who play on poor greens, I had developed a stroke with a rather long backswing from which I could hit the ball hard. Once I started playing on fast tournament greens as a professional this stroke let me down. I still used to swing the club too far back, but would then have to decelerate to try to keep the putt rolling slowly. It was only when I first played in top professional tournaments in 1976 that I came across fast greens. It took me a considerable length of time to adjust. Many people believe that I only really conquered my putting in 1985 when I won the Masters. In fact I had probably conquered most of my problems by 1983 after beginning to putt cross-handed.

The Cross-Handed Cure

My main difficulty in putting was that my right hand used to take over on short putts and jerk the putter head through. This is usually referred to as the 'yips'. Your right hand gets out of control and jerks the putter forward, pushing the ball out off line and often shooting it too far. The faster the green the more frightening this becomes. The difficulty, of course, if you putt badly is that it tends to put pressure on the rest of your game. I used to find myself hitting a good iron shot into the green perhaps 12 feet away, missing my putt for a birdie, and then would be under pressure on the next iron shot feeling that I had to get even closer to make my birdies. Bad putting puts pressure on chipping, pitching and the whole of the long game if you allow it to.

I soon realized that to become one of the best players in the world I had to conquer my putting difficulties. I was producing some good results but they didn't fully satisfy me. If I hadn't putted well as a youngster, and if I wasn't a good chipper and bunker player, I might have doubted that my hand–eye coordination was good enough to putt really well. But I knew that I had it in me, if I could only find the right technique and discover where I was going wrong.

There are two main principles, as we will see later, which seem to be common to the technique of most really good putters. **First, they usually keep a firm and consistent angle in the left arm and the left wrist through the whole stroke. Secondly, they manage to combine this with a light, sensitive grip pressure.** I found that with my usual stroke, setting the right hand below the left in the orthodox way, I couldn't keep my left wrist and arm working as a consistent unit *and* stay relaxed with this light grip pressure. If I relaxed, I was always aware of the left side breaking down through impact. As the angle of the wrist and arm altered I felt my club coming off line or the clubface turning. It seemed to allow

A common key for most good putters is the feeling of firmness in the left wrist throughout the stroke

20

the right hand to take over. If, on the other hand, I firmed up my left arm and wrist, it seemed to create too much tension.

I therefore decided that I had to find a method which would allow me to keep my left arm and wrist working smoothly as a unit without creating tension. A conventional grip always seemed to force me to bend the left wrist or elbow more than I wanted. I had occasionally seen other good players putting with a cross-handed grip and I decided that it might solve a lot of problems.

I use two quite distinct techniques for short-putting and long-putting. Short-putting to me, and to most tournament professionals, requires a precise stroke which must be absolutely repetitive. Distance is not much of a problem; what I want is an accurate stroke in which the putter moves back and forwards on the right line, returning the clubface absolutely square. Long-putting is very different. With a long putt the skill lies far more in being able to produce feel and sensitivity in your fingertips to get the ball running the right distance and in reading the greens really well. I therefore use a cross-handed method for my short putts, where I am working almost entirely on a repetitive stroke. For my long putts I use a more conventional method which gives me feel in my hands. There is a

The grips I use for short and long putts – cross-handed for firmness with the short, more conventional with the long for feel

distance somewhere between 15 and 25 feet at which I may use one method or the other. Sometimes a putt of 20 feet looks very straight and true and then I see a good short-putt stroke without any real difficulty in the line or length. If, on the other hand, the putt seems very fast or there is a big break, I may well decide that my other method is more appropriate to produce good touch. Sometimes with these medium-length putts I may set up one way and then change to the other style if I subsequently see the putt differently. I don't necessarily expect readers to follow my suggestions on cross-handed putting, but even with a conventional grip there must be two distinct approaches to short and long putts.

Short-Putting

My aim with a short putt, having read the green and found the line, is to stroke the ball right on the sweet spot of the putter and to set it rolling smoothly on the correct line. From about 15 feet and closer, distance should not be a problem. Obviously one has to get the correct distance, but usually that is secondary and much easier to achieve than getting the right line. With my short putts I want to strike the ball from the correct part of the clubface – the sweet spot – with the clubface perfectly square and the putter head travelling on line. I see good short-putting as being a question of swinging the putter head back and through on a perfectly straight line from ball to target. On putts of perhaps 5–6 feet or more I am aware of the putter head moving slightly inside this line on the backswing, but my predominant idea for short putts is to obtain a straight swing path.

I know, after hours of research and practice, that the key to my short-putting is to keep my left arm and left wrist as a constant unit. You will see this in nearly all really great putters. I achieve this by letting my left arm hang loosely and freely from the shoulder, and by gripping the club with the left hand very much to the side of the club, with the left thumb straight down the front of the putter. I always use a putter which has a flat-fronted grip. This helps in getting the hands in the right position, with the palms of both hands predominantly to the side of the club and the thumbs down the front. As I look down at my left hand I can see the left *thumb* running straight down the putter shaft, but *not* with the left *hand* on the top as in a conventional long-game grip. My right hand also holds the club with the palm to the side of the grip, never underneath it. Again, the thumb is virtually straight down the front of the grip and the right wrist and elbow are allowed to bend quite naturally. I use a form of reverse overlap grip, with my right index finger overlapping the little finger of my left hand and fitting snugly between the base of the little finger and the third finger. As I set up to the ball I have my eyes directly over the line from the ball to the hole, ensuring that they are never outside this line, with the ball halfway between the centre of my stance and my left instep and my hands very fractionally ahead of the ball. I like to use a fairly wide stance, with my feet about shoulder-width apart, aiming at stability and as little body movement as possible. My feeling is one of having the weight almost evenly distributed between left foot and right foot, but slightly favouring the left, and nicely balanced flat on the feet, neither towards the toes nor the heels.

The set-up has to be absolutely meticulous. It is essential that the clubface is set square to the desired direction. A degree or two out is no good at all. It must be square, with the putter head sitting flat on its sole. I then favour a perfectly square stance with the line across my toes parallel to the line of my putt. My feeling in the set-up is that I pull my right shoulder and right arm back just a shade into a square shoulder position.

Squareness at address, with the lines along the toes, shoulders and eyes all parallel to the putt

23

I feel the left arm and left hand are absolutely dominant, with the right arm, hand and indeed the shoulder in a passive position. I feel as though there is a complete unit, from my left shoulder through my left arm and hand and down into the putter, which controls the whole stroke. By setting up in this cross-handed position I am able to get rid of the unwanted feeling of the right hand being dominant. The whole stroke feels as though it can take place with the left arm perfectly in control.

My Routine

The set-up is vitally important in every part of the golf game and no less in putting. I am a great believer in following a specific routine for every single shot and sticking to it through thick and thin, whether in practice or in a tournament. I follow a rigid routine in putting just as I do in the rest of my golf. It may well be that my routine will change slightly over the years, but there is no doubt that I shall always have some form of routine which I shall stick to religiously.

My first stage, of course, is to read the green and to decide exactly where I want to hit the ball. Chapter 8 explains my systematic approach to this. It is crucial at this point that my decision is firm. If there is any doubt, then I will look again until my mind is clear. I then run through an absolutely repetitive procedure for lining up the putt. This exactness is important because it stops me hurrying or slowing down and ruining my stroke. Being meticulous in the pre-putt routine helps to produce a repetitive, consistent stroke because the muscles are activated in exactly the same way each time. I set up beside the ball and have one practice swing, during which I look at the hole in order to feel and imagine the distance. I then put the clubhead down behind the ball with my right hand, ensuring that the clubface is perfectly square. The head position is vital in seeing this squareness, and for me, like for most top professionals, it is essential that my eyes are directly over the ball to see this line. It is also very important to ensure that the line across the eyes is parallel to the line of the putt.

Having positioned the clubface squarely, I add the left hand to my grip and then take up my stance, ensuring again that the line across my shoulders is parallel to my putt. The line across my toes is square to slightly open, and of little concern compared with the shoulder line. I make sure I am comfortable and relaxed, the left arm hanging loose and straight and the right one tucked in.

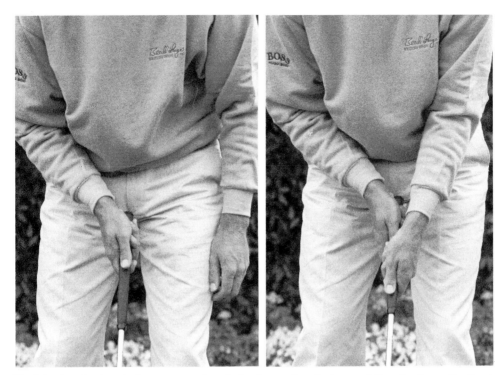

Positioning the hands for my cross-handed grip – palms facing and thumbs down the front of the putter

At this point the weight of the putter is quite definitely supported by my arms and *not* resting on the ground. I often hold the putter just clear of the ground. This encourages a smooth pendulum stroke. Resting the club on the ground can lead to a jerk as you gather up the weight of the club.

For my short putts I look up at the hole three times. This is a very important part of my routine and, again, I try religiously not to allow myself to alter this. It is tempting when you are doing well in a tournament to look up one more time to make quite certain that you have all the information you need. But allowing yourself to do this only leads to doubt and indecision. You can't gain anything from an extra look and all it does is to muddle your thinking. So I look up three times, no more and no less, for my short putts. In these three looks at the hole I am checking again the squareness of the putter blade, the line of my putt and pinpointing the exact spot at the front or edge of the hole where I intend to hit the ball. For very short putts these three looks can be out of the corner of my eye, but once I get a putt of 4–5 feet or more my head must obviously move. It is essential for me, and I would guess for most people, that the head turns in a swivelling action so that I look straight along the line. This gives me a far more accurate view of where I am going than it would if I lifted my head at all.

Having looked at my putt three times, I then focus my attention very firmly on the back of the ball and the precise spot I want to strike. I concentrate on swinging the putter head back on a straight line and through on a straight line, watching the ball intently but also being aware of the stroke. I never watch the putter head going back or through, other than occasionally in practice sessions, but most of the time I am aware of the stroke I am making. I mention this because I know that some top-class putters are almost entirely aware of the ball and the hole and virtually oblivious of the stroke. Gradually I have become more conscious of the ball, the hole and the way I want the ball to roll, and less aware of the movement of the putter. When I putted poorly I used at times to become mesmerized by the stroke, almost forgetting where the ball was going. I am sure that's what happens to a lot of club players.

The Putter Path

With short putts of perhaps 8 feet or less I have no feeling of the putter head moving back on an inside curve. I can feel that the stroke hinges from my left shoulder, that the putter head moves back on a perfectly straight line and the putter face stays looking slightly downwards as it swings back. As the putter head swings through I again feel it comes entirely from the left shoulder and arm, with the right side perfectly passive, the putter head moving through on this straight line, hitting the ball fractionally beyond the bottom of the swing and therefore slightly on the upswing, with the putter head stopping in a neat and tidy position a few inches beyond the spot where the ball was, and with the clubhead still perfectly square but now looking slightly upwards. There is no hinging in my left wrist or breaking down of the left arm whatsoever as this happens. In other words, it becomes a slightly under-and-up stroke, with the putter head moving in a saucer-shaped arc. I have no feeling at all of trying to keep the putter down particularly low in the backswing or in the throughswing, as this would be pulling the putter away from its natural arc centred on my left shoulder. What I am very conscious of is that the backswing and the throughswing mirror each other in both length and height. It is a symmetrical path and certainly, if anything, I would prefer the throughswing to be a little longer than the backswing.

My short-putting technique – the cross-handed grip allows me to keep my left wrist and arm as a constant unit, combined with relaxation

I like to be very conscious of the putter head, keeping a nice, constant pace through impact, accelerating slightly but without any trace of jerkiness. I have the feeling of hitting the ball slightly on the upswing. In Germany I used to pop the ball forward with a downward, jabbing stroke – a stroke you often see from players brought up on slow greens. Now I do exactly the reverse with my short putts and try to hit the ball fractionally on the upswing. The reason for this is twofold. First, in hitting the ball slightly on the upswing I achieve a slightly smoother roll to the ball. It probably helps reduce any unwanted jumping or sidespin on the ball, and also ensures that I keep the putter head moving on line towards the hole. I am very conscious of finishing the putt properly with the clubhead in a definite, stationary position. It stops quite definitely for one or two seconds, and I also try to ensure that I keep my head still for one or two seconds, almost hearing the ball drop rather than seeing it drop. Good putters tend to stay very still over their putts, and again, this is my way of staying still without creating unnecessary tension. It certainly wouldn't suit me to feel I was in any sort of locked position or static or rigid. My left arm is dominant and yet relaxed; my head and body stay still and yet relaxed.

Speed

My short-putting has gradually become more aggressive; my aim on any short putt would be for the ball, if it were to miss, to run approximately 15 inches past the hole. When I was a poor putter it used to worry me that I might miss the hole and have to face the putt back. Like most poor putters, I sometimes became cautious and used to trickle the ball at the hole, hoping that if it did miss it would at least stay a couple of inches away. **On bad greens a ball that is dying into the hole is likely to run off line more easily and miss. On good, fast greens a ball that is trickled towards the hole takes up far more break and you have to allow for more borrow.** I can now be far more aggressive and worry much less about what is going to happen if I should miss one. By being aggressive I can afford to hit the putt straighter, knowing it will hold its line. I am by no means as aggressive with my short putts as Tom Watson is, but I certainly try to attack the hole to ensure the ball holds its line. Obviously this depends on the green, but in principle my aim is to stop the ball about 15 inches past the hole for a missed putt.

When I started trying to adapt to good tournament greens I made the mistake, which I believe a lot of people make, of adopting a small, light putter. After some discussion with Seve Ballesteros I changed to a heavier putter and would now certainly favour a fairly heavy putter even on fast greens, with a slightly heavier one still on slow greens. The heavy putter enables me to stroke the ball without feeling that I have to hit it. As well as varying the weight of my putter, I am likely to vary the loft from one type of green to another. On fast greens I use a putter of 3–4 degrees of loft, and on slow greens, where there is a problem in getting the ball rolling properly, I move to a putter of 5–6 degrees. I like a putter which is long enough that I can stand up reasonably tall and yet short enough that I can feel my left arm hanging loosely and freely, with my right hand still virtually at the end of the grip. At my height, 5 feet 8 inches (173 cm), I feel most comfortable with a 34-inch putter.

My whole key with short-putting is the feeling of my left arm being a unit and thoroughly in control, with my eyes directly over the line of the putt and the putter head swinging back and forth on a straight line. I feel that both arms and the putter move as one piece throughout. I concentrate on returning the sweet spot of the putter directly to the back of the ball, striking the ball fractionally on the upswing, at a consistent height, without making contact with the ground at any point during the stroke.

Long-Putting

My long-putting technique is quite orthodox in that I use a fairly conventional grip rather than a cross-handed one. As I have said, there is sometimes a point between about 15 and 25 feet at which I may at first be in two minds as to which method to use. But once I get beyond 25 feet I am invariably working at acquiring a feeling for distance and good judgement, rather than worrying about direction and being precise and accurate with my stroke. I don't wish to sound misleading in suggesting that the stroke is not important, because, of course, it is. But as a rule it is the distance and exact judgement of the strength of the putt that are so crucial. Failure with long putts – by which I mean a putt which isn't left within a foot or so of the hole – is far more a question of a poorly read putt or of badly gauged distance than one in which the line and stroke haven't been good enough.

Having systematically read the putt, I make a practice swing in which I try to visualize the distance involved and rehearse the length of the backswing and throughswing. All too often I see my pro-am partners making practice swings for long putts which bear no resemblance to the swing they make with the ball. This practice swing is important in giving my body the clue to the length of swing and speed of the roll I want with the ball.

I look at a putt and imagine a curve on the green along which the ball will travel. I then pick a definite spot either at the same distance as the hole or somewhere en route to it, and aim at that, knowing that the ball will break away from it. If the putt is likely only to break a fairly small amount, perhaps 18 inches or so at the most, then I will usually choose a spot at the same distance as the hole and aim at that. If there is a very big break, like the greens at Augusta, then I am far more likely to choose a spot on the way to the hole and see the putt as almost forming a triangle.

Again, I keep to a rigid routine in setting up to the ball. In adopting my grip I ensure that I set the clubhead square to my aiming point. In my long-putting grip – right hand below left – the little finger of my right hand overlaps the second finger of the left, with the left index finger pointing straight down the back of the other three fingers of the right. As before, my eyes are directly over the line from the ball to the hole and I concentrate on keeping my body still. I generally look up four times for a long putt rather than the three times for a short putt. There is a temptation amongst amateur golfers to look up more often the longer the putt. However, I almost always limit myself to four looks, unless the putt requires an extremely complex line, and ensure that I have a good picture in my mind of the exact putt. In many ways the more instinctive I allow myself to be over the long-putting, the more accurate I am. I know from experience that if I start looking up too often I only muddle my thinking and get caught between two thoughts.

My stance for long-putting is again fairly wide, with the weight almost evenly planted on both feet, perhaps slightly favouring the left, and perfectly balanced from heel to toe. With my right hand below my left hand in this fairly orthodox grip the right shoulder is naturally much farther below the left shoulder than in my short-putting. The right hand now comes into play far more than with the short putts in that I produce feel and sensitivity for the distance in the fingers of the left hand and the first three fingers and thumb of my right. **When I am putting well my grip seems light and sensitive, and I easily transfer the feeling from my fingers right through to my putter head, feeling the ball coming off the clubface in a very soft and delicate manner.** This is something you have to work on to be able to produce the same feel under the pressures of tournament golf. Again, it is essential to stay relaxed to be able to produce a really great touch in tournament golf.

My long-putting address position

The long-putting grip

It would be wrong to suggest that in long-putting the stroke is not important. It is vital in many ways, particularly in ensuring that the ball is contacted with the right part of the clubface – the sweet spot – and also at a consistent depth on the clubface, neither thinning it nor making even the slightest contact with the ground. This accurate strike on the clubface is necessary to set the ball running properly with consistent speed. But the actual stroke does not need to be so precise. Now, instead of a straight line, the putter head very definitely follows a curved inside path on the backswing. This is just like in the long game. Once I swing the putter more than just a few inches it feels as though it needs to come back on an inside curve. I would have to compensate if I tried to keep it swinging in a straight line for my long putts. I therefore allow the putter head to move quite freely on a curved arc, and, in truth, I concentrate far more on striking the back of the ball and setting it rolling in the right direction at the right speed, than on thinking about the path of the clubhead. This is another reason why I have benefited so much from adopting a cross-handed grip with my short putts and a fairly conventional one with my long putts. It has meant that I adopt two quite distinct methods and that I don't get caught somewhere between one and the other.

My long-putting is aimed at perfect touch. Sometimes I set up to the ball and seem to have a wonderful feeling of knowing exactly how it is going to roll, easily visualizing it dropping into the right part of the hole. I have a fairly aggressive approach, trying to hole most long putts, except for those which are exceedingly sidehill or downhill, but at the same time being very aware of where I want to leave the ball just in case I should miss – perhaps to leave myself an uphill rather than a downhill putt on the return.

My long-putt technique centres on producing good feel through my fingers and right thumb, reading the greens well and, as with my short putts, adopting and sticking to a rigid routine to create muscle memory for a repetitive stroke.

2 The Principles of Putting

It would obviously be untrue to suggest that all top-class professionals agree over the techniques they employ with the long game. But there is certainly considerably more agreement over our ideas on the long game and on most aspects of the short game than there is over putting. If you search for any sort of common ground in putting methods you are likely to find contradictions in virtually everything. Some players suggest that you should stand upright, others that you should crouch. Some use a predominantly left-hand method, others a right. For anyone trying to improve his putting the different opinions are confusing. At the end of the day you come to the conclusion that good putters find their method more by trial and error than by following definite guidelines.

Long-Game Logic

Correcting problems in the long game can be done in a systematic and perfectly logical way. If, for example, I go out on the practice ground and find myself hitting iron shots slightly left of target, I can follow a definite pattern in correcting the error. First of all I would look carefully at the flight of the ball, and this would lead logically back with a little experimentation to find the error at impact. The flight of the ball with the long game tells us a lot. A ball which finishes left of target with an iron shot can get there by several routes. It may be that I am pulling the ball so that it flies in a straight line to the left. It may be that I am drawing it to the left, in other words starting straight on target but with the ball spinning and bending to the left. I might have a combination of a slight pull and a draw. I might be starting the ball slightly right of target and hooking it back to the left. As soon as I see the flight of the ball I can tell myself quite logically what has happened at impact. If the ball starts left or right, then I know my attack at impact is directed slightly left or right. I can adjust the ball position or simply redirect that attack to make the correction. If the ball bends away to the left in flight, then I know I am

In the long game the flight of the ball indicates what has happened at impact. Correcting a problem can be logical and systematic. A putt which misses doesn't usually provide such clear feedback. It can be caused in so many ways getting a little sidespin on the ball with the clubface closing relative to the line of my swing. This would give me certain clues about checking my grip, clubface, alignment and so on.

In the long game the good professional coach works from what he sees in the flight of each shot and makes the pupil understand the mechanics involved so that he can himself work through a logical process to improvement. For good players it is the flight of the ball that tells them virtually everything. Obviously they don't all swing the golf club in the same way, but when one analyses what happens in the hitting area there is not that much difference between good players. Some like to aim at hitting a ball dead straight. Others like to feel the shots always fading slightly from left to right. And some, myself included, usually like to feel that the ball draws a little from right to left. This is what gives us our slightly different approaches to the game and results in fairly minor differences in technique in regard to grip, stance, the plane and so on. With short shots round the green much the same applies. We can look at the flight of the ball, see what happens, and then logically work out any correction needed at impact and, in turn, in the swing. But once we get on to putting, and particularly with short-putting, the story is very different.

The Missed Putt

With the long game most tournament professionals know exactly what has caused a faulty flight to a shot. With putting this simply is not true. I explained above what I would read into a long shot which missed the target to the left. But if I miss a 4-foot putt to the left it can be caused by any of the following:

1. The putter face may have been closed just 1–2 degrees.
2. I may not have hit the ball with the sweet spot of the putter, but slightly towards the heel, allowing the putter face to close.
3. I may have read the putt wrongly and there may have been a break I hadn't noticed.
4. I may have pulled the putt with the putter moving in a left-aimed direction.
5. I may not have sent the putt rolling truly, so that it did not hold its line.
6. I may have had downright bad luck, the ball hitting a little spike mark or other irregularity and turning away.

My coach and great friend, Willi Hoffman, helping me look for real precision with a putt. Why did it miss, Willi? What did it do?

If you miss a shortish putt you are not necessarily aware of the error. Quite often you will see tournament professionals missing putts and looking at their caddies in astonishment for some clue as to what went wrong. Obviously we practise putting a great deal, but even at our standard we cannot always be absolutely certain why a putt has missed. In the long game you get an entirely different type of flight on the ball with a slightly closed clubface than you do with a slightly left-aimed attack. With a putt you don't see any difference and won't necessarily know what went wrong. For this reason I'm sure that for most people learning to be a good putter is far more a question of trial and error than of logic and analysis. With the long game you are more likely to get a specific pattern of shots so that the error is a fairly consistent one. With putting players who have difficulty often seem to hit bad putts in a fairly random manner, never quite knowing whether they are misreading the putt or mis-striking it.

Science or Inspiration

Many of the unusual putting methods that can be seen are probably adopted through trial and error with no real rhyme or reason. The player might turn one foot in or out, adjust his weight distribution or his head position in the search for something which works, without really knowing why. If a few more putts than usual are successful, he probably attributes the fact to this change. It may not be the reason at all but it simply gives him confidence.

In some ways short-putting is scientific and precise; in other ways it is very subjective and more a question of feel, confidence and a good eye. Several people have tried to make putting machines to test theories on putting. Even a putting machine with an entirely repetitive movement is not 100 per cent reliable on as near perfect a green as can be achieved. There are little inexplicable discrepancies from time to time. Indeed, if you look at two of the greatest golfers who ever lived, Bobby Jones and Jack Nicklaus, both seem to suggest that putting cannot be truly scientific. Bobby Jones, who was apparently a great putter, said that there was little hope of reducing putting to a science and that it was virtually a waste of time and energy to try to perfect a putting stroke. I don't go along with that, but obviously there are or have been great putters who have relied

Opposite: Jack Nicklaus willing a putt on its way. 'Putting,' he once wrote, 'is inspiration and not mechanical'

more on a good eye and a sensitive touch than on a precise and well-rehearsed method. Nicklaus in his book *The Greatest Game of All** openly admits that putting is the least scientific and mechanical part of his game. He says that he does just about anything to make a putt drop, changing his set-up and method not just from day to day but from green to green. 'Putting,' he writes, 'is inspiration and not mechanical.' His book was written in 1969 but presumably his thoughts remain the same.

Some great champions are probably born with a marvellous eye for putting. Providing they never lose confidence from a bad patch on the greens, they can rely on their excellent judgement and natural feel. I started out with a very good eye for putting. As a youngster I never thought twice about holing short putts and my friends in Germany always assumed I would hole everything from 6 feet or less. But when I moved to the fast tournament greens my confidence was shattered and I had to start all over again.

We can and must be precise and methodical over putting, certainly from distances up to 20 feet or so. When Bobby Jones was in his heyday he probably putted on greens much like those I was brought up on, with a not particularly good surface and certainly nowhere near as fast as today's tournament greens. Nowadays tournament officials are very exact over the way in which the greens are prepared. The speed of the greens is measured accurately with a gadget called a stimpmeter. This piece of apparatus is designed to set a ball rolling down an inclined plane of uniform length measuring the distance it rolls from the bottom to give an assessment of speed. The mower cutting height can then be adjusted to produce the exact speed required. Good greenkeepers and tournament officials are very precise over their preparation; the better the greens the more precise we need to be over our methods.

The Five Principles of Putting

Any golfer can improve his putting, often quite dramatically, with a good, sound understanding of the principles involved. All good putters follow these principles. They all have certain aims even though they may achieve them in completely different ways. The principles of putting are as follows:

* *The Greatest Game of All*, Jack Nicklaus (Simon and Schuster, 1969)

1. The putter face should be square at address and at impact.
2. The putter must be travelling on target at the moment of impact.
3. The depth and angle of strike must be correct to set the ball rolling well.
4. The putter head must be travelling at the right speed at impact to produce the desired distance.
5. The overall stroke needs to be repetitive for consistency.

In summary, you should always aim for:

1.	**Square clubface**	4.	**Speed and distance**
2.	**Direction at impact**	5.	**Repetitive stroke**
3.	**Perfect roll**		

Whatever you work at in putting, you should have these five aims clearly in mind. I hope they are self-explanatory. Let us run through them very briefly and then, in the next chapters, look at how others achieve them and how best you can achieve them.

First, it goes without saying that the clubface should be square, i.e. directly facing your target, at address and return there at impact. If the putter face is 1 degree out for a 6-foot putt the ball will be $1\frac{1}{4}$ inches off line as it hits the hole and will often spin out. It needs to be absolutely exact. Secondly, you need to have the putter travelling directly on target at impact. Just as with the long game, the ball will start in the direction of the strike. As I explained above, in the long game clubface errors and direction-of-attack errors cause quite different flights. In putting, they result in virtually the same error and are often indistinguishable. Thirdly, the ball must roll well by being struck from the sweet spot to hold its line and produce consistent distance. You need to strike the back of the ball at a consistent depth on the clubface, with the clubhead about a quarter of an inch from the ground to keep it rolling smoothly. Fourthly, and most importantly, the speed of the attack has to be correct to produce the distance you want. Fifthly, the stroke needs to be as simple and repetitive as possible to withstand tournament pressure and eliminate as many variables as possible.

3 The Schools of Thought

In the search for a putting method is there any one thing that the best tournament professionals agree over? Without doubt each will agree with my five principles of putting, but they will by no means agree on how we achieve them. We can't agree whether we stand up tall or bend right over. We can't agree whether we use a straight-back-and-through putting path or see it as a curve. In various instructional books you will find great players advocating virtually everything. In looking for a route to precision putting I believe we have to consider all these schools of thought and try to come to some conclusion. We need to see how certain bits of advice go with certain other bits of advice. There is no point extracting one little piece of information from one good player and linking it with information from another good player if the two are quite incompatible. That would be like having a golf swing made up of Jack Nicklaus's backswing and Lee Trevino's followthrough! So where do we start?

Head Position

Let us start where there is least disagreement. **Almost without doubt good putters suggest we adopt an address position in which the line of the eyes is directly over the ball–target line.** From this position it is generally assumed that you have the best possible view of that line, both for seeing the putt and for setting the putter face squarely to it. **What most top players do, but what is not so frequently stressed, is keep the line of the eyes perfectly parallel with the putt.** From this position the head should ideally be able to swivel, rather than lifting and turning, to look from the ball to the hole and back again. To achieve this swivelling most good putters, whether they stand up tall or bend over, have the head in a fairly low position so that the face is virtually horizontal. From here you can swivel. With the head up there is a tendency to turn and lift. I would guess we are unanimous in suggesting that this is where the head

My head swivelling, *not* lifting and turning, to view a short putt, head horizontal, eyes parallel to the line of the putt

should be even though we don't all necessarily follow it. I have never known a good player suggest that the eyes should be outside the line of the putt. There are some who do this, perhaps unwittingly, but certainly for most people it would make vision very difficult, and the general theory is that it tends to make you pull the ball to the left. There are players who have the head slightly inside this line. Ben Crenshaw seems to be fractionally inside. Isao Aoki and Fuzzy Zoeller are very definitely inside. So to a far lesser extent is Peter Thomson. In Aoki's case one assumes that he sees a straight line far more accurately with his eyes inside the ball–target line than with his head directly over it.

Fuzzy Zoeller, whose eyes are usually well inside the ball at address rather than directly above it, head horizontal to swivel not lift

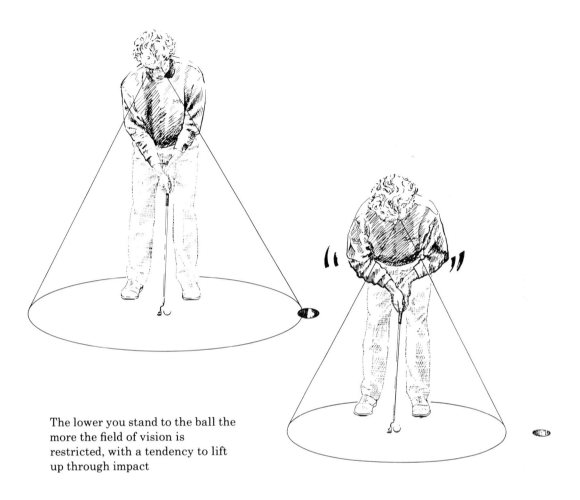

The lower you stand to the ball the
more the field of vision is
restricted, with a tendency to lift
up through impact

The area where there is some difference of opinion over head position
is the height at which you hold it and the degree to which you bend over.
There are a number of very tall professionals who bend over a long way.
Andy North and Johnny Miller are prime examples of players who get
very low to the ball. Possibly their eyes feel more comfortable in focusing
on the ball and seeing the line of the putt in this position. However, the
difficulty if you get too low is that you gradually restrict your field of
peripheral vision in the direction of the hole, and there is a tendency to
get the head too much outside the line of the putt. Most putters who set
up bent right over tend to have the arms bent and tucked in. From here
the left arm and wrist are more likely to be bending and folding through
the stroke. Players who stand up fairly tall to the ball, providing they still
have their head over, are usually in a position in which the arms can hang

Andy North – right over the ball but with both arms fairly straight

fairly straight and stay as a constant unit through the stroke. Andy North is the exception to this. He bends right over and yet hangs his arms straight using a very short putter.

Straight Path or Curved Path

Let us look first at short putts, those up to 6 feet or so. There are two entirely different schools of thought about the putter path and the way in which the clubface is returned squarely to the ball. Remember that we want the clubface square and the putter travelling in the right direction. With a short putt some players very definitely see the putter head travelling back and through on a straight line. With this kind of action the putter face is kept square to the stroke, turning under and therefore looking slightly downwards as it swings back, and staying square to the line and looking slightly upwards as it swings through. This is the feeling I have for a short putt. You will usually see this type of stroke from players who stand up fairly well at address, swinging their arms and club as a unit, and who are probably fairly left-side dominant in their action. Players are often recommended to swing the putter straight back and through on a line without the proviso that this really only applies to fairly short putts. There must also be the proviso that the putter is fairly upright in lie, probably with a high hand position and the stroke coming predominantly from the shoulders. The straight-back-and-through path certainly would not go hand in hand with an address like Fuzzy Zoeller's with the head inside the line of the putt and the hands low.

A straight-back-and-through path for shortish putts, usually needing a fairly upright putter and stance. The putter face stays looking at the hole throughout

The putter face works quite differently with a curved path,
turning with the path of the putter. Some professionals use this
for long and short putts. I prefer a straight-back-and-through
path for short ones

The other school of thought holds an entirely different view. To them
the putter must always work back on a slight curve, however short the
putt, with the clubface quite naturally rotating slightly so that it stays
square to that path. Some people suggest that in the straight-back-and-
through path the clubface is 'hooded' and that in the inside curve it is
opened. I don't go along with that. Certainly the putter face moves differently but it simply stays square to the path you are using. Both can be
achieved quite easily without any independent wrist movement. Again,
you cannot say that one or the other is right. Certainly this type of slightly
curved path is more likely to be seen from players who have a lower
address position, with perhaps more emphasis on the forearms, wrists and
hands than on a movement from the shoulders. On the other hand, when
you look at Ben Crenshaw and Bob Charles, who both swing predominantly from the shoulders, they quite definitely swing the club back
slightly on an inside path even for short putts. Some instructional books
talk as though one method is right and the other is wrong. Some advocate
one and some the other. Both have their merits, providing you adopt one
singlemindedly and don't get caught with a combination of the two.

In moving on to longer putts, it seems inevitable that the clubhead must
start coming back on a curved path, whatever the player does with a short
putt. **As putts become longer the stroke gradually begins to take on
the characteristics of the long game and to move quite naturally
inside on a curved path.** In the long game this cannot help but happen

A picture of intense concentration and sheer determination

Auf wiedersehen!

A little more body movement than I would recommend!

Hubert Green proving that just about anything goes

because of the distance you stand from the ball. In putting it is in theory quite possible for the putter head to continue to swing back and forth on an entirely straight line. Again, this is only likely to happen with a player who has a particularly high hand position at address and who uses the most upright putter allowed. The very fact of having the hands inside the line of the putt must inevitably bring the putter head back inside as the stroke lengthens, unless there is some definite compensatory movement and the wrists begin to turn under. There are undoubtedly one or two good professionals who continue to adopt a very straight-line approach on their long putting. But we are virtually unanimous in saying that at some point the putter must adopt a curve and the clubface stay square to that curve. Our difference of opinion is the point at which this happens and it is on the short putts that our approach differs. Later, when discussing short-putt precision, we will look at my ideas for determining which method is likely to suit you.

Upswing or Downswing

In the long game we have to use three different kinds of attack on a golf ball. Certain shots, namely those with the short and medium irons, those from bad or hanging lies, require a downward attack. Fairway woods and long irons from standard lies can be nipped off at the very bottom of the swing, and a driver requires an upward contact from beyond the bottom of the swing. Good players have to use all three as and when the need arises. There may be an odd shot that we see differently. A 4-wood from a tight lie might suggest to one player a sweeping contact and to another a more downward contact. But in general we would agree over what we are trying to achieve and roughly the way in which we achieve it. In putting there are quite different opinions as to what is right and what is wrong. The difference, of course, is that we are not trying to loft the ball and so, whether, within limits, we hit down or up on the ball or hit it at the bottom of the swing, the ball simply rolls along the ground. Again, it is all too easy to suggest that one approach is right and the other wrong, when in reality each has its merits, providing once more that we know which we are adopting and why we are adopting it.

Some players clearly see the putting stroke as being a downward attack. Gary Player and Isao Aoki are two examples of excellent putters who give the ball a fairly sharp, downward rap. Possibly this is produced from being brought up in South Africa and Japan respectively where the greens have

Isao Aoki, who uses a sharp, downward strike, stopping almost at the moment of impact. With his eyes well inside the line of the putt, hands low, toe of the putter off the ground, it shows that anything goes providing it works!

a lot of grain and often need an extra degree of firmness to start the ball on its way. But here again, it is not a hard-and-fast rule. South African Bobby Locke, whom many still regard as one of the greatest putters of all time, worked hard at producing an upward strike to the ball. In his view this sets the ball rolling smoothly and keeps it holding its line. I doubt that there are many top-class professionals who strike the ball with a downward action unless faced with particularly slow or rough greens. A downward stroke pops the ball forward rather than rolls it smoothly. My own feeling is one of a horizontal to slightly upward strike. Sandy Lyle and Ben Crenshaw do the same, and Tom Watson has a very markedly upward movement beyond the ball, catching it either at the very bottom of the swing or fractionally on the upswing. On the other hand, Jack Nicklaus has in the past suggested that the perfect putting stroke makes contact with the ball at the very bottom of the swing, going so far as to say that no really good putters strike the ball on the upswing. He may have changed his view on this in recent years.

Sandy Lyle, striking the ball with a definite upward movement to produce the feeling of rolling the ball perfectly

Once again, you can see that there are completely contrasting schools of thought. The player who has putting difficulties can read one point of view stated quite dogmatically and then find just the opposite stated as strongly.

Right Side or Left Side

Is putting right-side or left-side dominated? Once again we differ in our views over putting far more than over the long game. The long game requires the perfect blend of left side and right side to produce control and power. There is a general consensus of opinion that the backswing and the start of the downswing have to be very left-side dominant, with the right producing power to the shot. In putting the requirements for a short putt simply involve swinging the putter head along a line or through a curve 12–15 inches in length. You can achieve this in many different ways and, again, the player who is searching for real guidelines can find one player describing it as entirely left-side dominant, another thinking of it as a right-handed action, and others who see it as a perfect blending of the two.

Certainly we are not unanimous in our views, but I would suggest that it is a very widely accepted principle that the left wrist and left arm should swing as a constant unit through the stroke without breaking down and in the process possibly pulling the clubhead off line. To achieve this the left arm has to be set in either a straight position whether firm or hanging loose, or set firmly with a precise angle to the elbow and the wrist. To maintain this for short putts, many of the best putters see the left arm as being all-important and dominant both back and through. Certainly my feeling on short-putting is of left-side control, and there are many professionals who advocate practising putting with only the left arm to develop this feeling. Player, Locke and Trevino are all fine putters who have emphasized the role of the left arm and its feeling of dominance and control, with the right hand contributing sensitivity and distance judgement.

Others clearly set themselves up with both arms working together as a unit so that there is no breakdown in the angle of either arm. This is noticeable in players like Bob Charles, Ben Crenshaw and Seve Ballesteros, who appear to stress a constant unit of both arms rather than one or the other. There are also those who suggest that the stroke is a combination of the two, being back with the left and through with the right.

Still others see the putting stroke as being thoroughly right-handed. Palmer and Nicklaus, who are amongst the greatest putters of all time, have each described the stroke as being mainly right-handed. Palmer suggested that the right hand is ready to roll the ball with precision. Nicklaus too favoured the dominance of the right hand and the importance of the position of the right arm and wrist rather than the left. This action has been copied very successfully by Johnny Miller, who believes that the left arm never dominates in putting or the long game but simply follows on if the right hand is working well. What is perhaps apparent in all these players is that the right shoulder is carried fairly low at address, meaning that the dominance of the right hand is likely to produce an under-and-up movement. Extreme right-hand dominance from a fairly horizontal shoulder line could all too easily pull the club off line. Casper stressed the sensitive feel to the right hand, with the reservation that the left hand steadied the stroke and worked to keep the clubface square – much the same approach as Lee Trevino's.

Wrists or No Wrists

Here, very fortunately, we are beginning to find areas where there is less disagreement amongst the top players. Without doubt everyone sees the wrists as having some part to play in long putts. They are needed to produce sufficient momentum to get the ball travelling the right length. There is also little doubt in my mind that the putting stroke used to be seen as far more wristy than it is now. Hagen was undoubtedly wristy by modern standards. Bobby Jones reputedly used more hand and wrist action than we do now. But it was not just in the 1920s and 1930s that more wrist action was employed. Both Arnold Palmer and Billy Casper, perhaps the two best putters of the 1960s, employed considerable wrist action for short putts as well as for long. Palmer's knock-kneed address position locked his body perfectly still. His arms stayed virtually motionless and the wrists hinged to push the putter back on line and hinged to bring it through again. Casper was less wristy but the technique was on much the same line. Presumably at the time it was followed avidly by other professionals and by amateurs trying to achieve the same results.

Now most professionals try to eliminate wrist action, trying to adopt styles like those of Bob Charles, Ben Crenshaw, Ray Floyd and Tom Watson, in which the whole method works to avoid any possible breakdown by minimizing movement in the wrists. The change in styles is probably the result of the change in playing conditions. Tournament greens are

Bobby Jones – a hands and wrists method typical of the 1920s and 1930s, emphasizing relaxation, head and eyes naturally turning to follow the ball. One of the few players who didn't advocate a steady head

Arnold Palmer, knees knocked in, body motionless, with the wrists hinging back and through

presumably far better prepared and far faster than they were fifty years ago, and lend themselves to a firm, wrist-free action. In America this is the style predominantly taught and used by the top players. On the slow, comparatively rougher greens of the Far East, Africa and northern Europe players are more likely to use a wristier style.

Relaxation and Stability

We now come to the one area in putting where there seems to be virtual agreement among the game's finest putters. Almost without exception there is a clear suggestion that the head and body should remain absolutely still throughout the putting stroke, eliminating any tendency to look up before the moment of impact or to sway towards the hole. Unlike other areas of putting technique, there has been no change in fashion or thoughts on this point throughout the years.

Harry Vardon advised that 'unquestionably the most important

Tom Watson, with the left wrist and arm
firm and constant throughout

My own cross-handed approach,
the left wrist straight but relaxed

**principle in putting is to keep the head and body absolutely still
during the stroke.' It is a piece of advice repeated time and time
again with considerable emphasis. Any putting stroke needs to be
repetitive and a player must undoubtedly work at this principle of
keeping the head and body absolutely still.**

Some golfers, like Palmer and Player, quite clearly adopt address positions which are tightly locked to ensure that there is no movement at all
in the head. Palmer knocks his knees and turns in his toes to produce a
rigid set-up position. Gary Player can be seen holding his head perfectly
still for an exaggeratedly long period of time, often well after the ball has
dropped into the hole or has obviously missed and stopped. Nicklaus
appears to set up in a very firm, stable position, again with the thought
quite clearly in his mind of avoiding any tendency to sway or move his
head throughout the stroke. Positions like those of Palmer and Player seem
to show considerable rigidity and tension. This tension would certainly not
suit me.

There are those, on the other hand, who emphasize the need to be
perfectly relaxed throughout the putting stroke. The difficulty lies in
achieving both together, staying still and yet being relaxed. Bobby Jones

Gary Player – a very firm, rigid stance, head and eyes motionless until the ball drops

went so far as to say that it was a mistake to advise a golfer to keep his body still when putting because, in his view, it was impossible to be quite still and yet relaxed. He seems to be the one great golfer who goes so far as to emphasize relaxation at the expense of keeping the head perfectly still. Others tend to emphasize both and the importance of blending one with the other.

We undoubtedly differ in the way we relate relaxation to the grip. Many players suggest the grip must be very light and delicate, while others emphasize a degree of firmness in the wrists and the grip itself, with the object of keeping the putter blade square through the stroke. Bobby Locke said that you should hold the putter so lightly 'that it nearly drops from your hands'. Perhaps this is an extreme view, but certainly the lightness of the grip, combined with just the right degree of firmness, is stressed by players like Trevino, Crenshaw and Ballesteros, who emphasize sensitivity and feel. Tom Watson, on the other hand, appears to hold the club fairly firmly with his left hand, aiming at a method whereby hand and wrist action in the stroke are virtually eliminated.

Although there seems to be agreement that the head should be kept perfectly still with as little body movement as possible, how we achieve this combined with a degree of relaxation is not agreed. For the golfer in search of a good putting technique and an answer to his or her putting problems, it is perhaps of little comfort that there is such a lack of agreement between the game's greatest putters. Virtually every piece of advice put forward by one player can be met with entirely contrary advice by another. One school of thought dogmatically takes one point of view and another stresses quite the opposite. I believe it is essential in learning to putt well that one explores each of these schools of thought to link up the different opinions given and to see how they match one to another. In this way it is possible to avoid plucking advice from here and there when the principles are not compatible. Without this understanding the student is quite likely to take one piece of advice from one player and one from another without realizing that the underlying assumptions on technique are from very different schools of thought. Remember what I said about trying to adopt Jack Nicklaus's backswing and Lee Trevino's follow-through!

Sometimes in your search for a winning putting stroke you will find the conflicting pieces of advice confusing and discouraging. But once you have unravelled all the information you will be able to see which schools of thought suit you and to piece the advice together to form your own method.

4 Contrasting Styles

The styles of some of the world's top players show considerable differences. Any reader in search of a putting style to suit himself or herself should be able to follow the principles set out in the rest of this book and see in one or more of the great players a style with which he can identify.

Bobby Locke

Unfortunately I am too young to have seen Bobby Locke in action. All I know of his technique is what I have read in books and seen from pictures. He was obviously regarded by many as the greatest putter in the game but with a technique which was unique. It seems that his whole sense of purpose in putting was to set the ball rolling perfectly truly with what he described as top spin. He used the same hickory-shafted blade putter throughout his career, the shaft apparently being somewhat longer than standard and his hands always gripping right at the top of the shaft. Locke played all his long-game shots with a hook or a draw, and he saw his putting in much the same way. He used the same standard Vardon grip for putting that he used for the rest of his game, with the one alteration of setting the thumbs straight down the front of the shaft. He then adopted a very narrow, closed position with the right foot behind the left, ball opposite the left foot, with the aim of striking the ball slightly on the upswing to impart added top spin. Another idiosyncrasy of Locke's method was to address the ball on the toe of the club, which in his view made it easier to take the putter head back inside the line of the putt. Locke's stroke was built around taking the putter back as low as possible on an inside path, seemingly hooding the clubface by turning his left wrist slightly under in the backswing. In his stroke Locke emphasized the importance of keeping the putter head travelling slowly and smoothly and keeping his own head down and still until the ball was well on its way. In his putting stance it was clear that his head and upper back were well over the ball, the neck and back of his head being virtually horizontal.

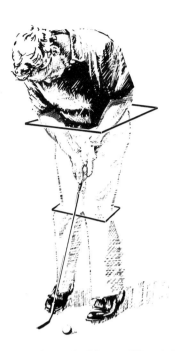

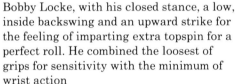

Bobby Locke, with his closed stance, a low, inside backswing and an upward strike for the feeling of imparting extra topspin for a perfect roll. He combined the loosest of grips for sensitivity with the minimum of wrist action

Arnold Palmer, 'holding still' with his knock-kneed set-up, left wrist hinging back, ready to hinge the putter through with the right

From this position he was able to swivel his head to look along the line of the putt without any tendency to look up and sway forward. Locke's putting was built around sensitivity and feel in his hands, with an extremely loose grip. Although he stressed the importance of looseness in the grip, he also emphasized the importance of eliminating wrist action in the stroke.

Arnold Palmer

Nicklaus described Palmer in his heyday as the greatest putter he had ever seen. Palmer's method is quite different from that adopted by most of today's tournament professionals. He said at one time that the mechanical side of putting was hardly worth mentioning; the only mechanical secret to putting was what he termed 'holding still'. His whole stance and method were aimed at achieving just this. He adopted a knock-kneed position, with his toes turned inward, in order to lock his body into position and to

Nicklaus described Palmer in his heyday as the greatest putter he had ever seen

keep his head perfectly still. Palmer was a wrist putter. On the short putts he kept not only his whole body but also his arms virtually motionless, hinging the putter back and forward, with a turning under of the left wrist and hand on the backswing, the right hand rolling the ball through from there with precision. The putter face looked down on the backswing and up on the throughswing, with a minimum of movement except in the hands and wrists. To Palmer in his days of winning championships there was apparently little more to putting than remaining perfectly motionless and attacking each putt with confidence.

Billy Casper

Casper, like Palmer, was primarily a hand and wrist putter. Although he was obviously a very fine striker of the ball, most of his contemporaries considered that it was the excellence of his putting that enabled him to win five Vardon trophies for heading the USPGA scoring averages. Indeed, Hogan allegedly said of Casper that if he couldn't putt he'd have been outside the ropes at a tournament selling hot dogs! Whether the statement

Billy Casper, another of the game's greatest ever putters, with such a simple wrist-hinging method, the ball unusually close to the feet, clubface square to the hole throughout

was ever made or not, it does show what Casper's fellow professionals thought of his touch on the green.

Casper stood well up to the ball, with it positioned much closer to his feet than usual. He stood relatively upright, yet with his head held in a horizontal position, thus enabling him to swivel his head rather than lift or turn it. He used a very standard reverse overlapping grip for putting, keeping the club more in the fingers of his left hand than many players did, improving the feel in his fingers. In the set-up Casper stressed the alignment of his upper body and yet surprisingly varied his foot position from time to time, with it sometimes open and sometimes closed, but with the ball always played just inside his left heel. His hand position at address was somewhat unusual, the hands being particularly close to his legs, with the left hand and arm almost brushing his left thigh at times. For Casper the stroke was controlled by his left hand, both in pushing the club back and pulling the putter through, but his exceptional touch came from the right hand. For short putts his putting stroke was very much like that of Palmer, hinging the putter back with his wrists and hinging it through with his wrists, only adding arm movement for putts of perhaps 15–18 feet or more. As with any putting stroke predominantly using hand and wrist action, Casper's putter lifted noticeably upwards in the backswing but with a slightly downward strike keeping it relatively low on the throughswing. Casper stressed the feel in his hands, staying perfectly relaxed and concentrating on setting the ball rolling smoothly for the first few inches.

Bob Charles

Bob Charles, the New Zealand left-hander, shows the complete reverse of the methods used by Palmer and Casper. He relies on the arms and shoulders, without any hand and wrist action whatsoever. Like the majority of great putters, he uses a reverse overlap grip, with the palms of the hands facing and the thumbs straight down the front of the grip. He uses equal pressure in both hands to encourage them to work completely together and never in opposition. Unlike Casper, who saw the alignment of the feet as relatively unimportant, Charles stresses the importance of a totally square relationship, the lines across his feet, body and shoulders being absolutely parallel to the line of the putt. His head too is held in a perfectly horizontal position, eyes directly over the ball, with emphasis on the club shaft pointing straight up towards him.

Charles stresses the feeling of a pendulum, moving his arms and shoulders and the putter as a solid unit, pivoted from the centre of his neck. In

Bob Charles, quite the opposite to Palmer and Casper, relying on a pivoting from the shoulders, with the arms, wrists and hands working as a unit this way he sees the pendulum stroke as bringing the putter head back quite naturally on a slightly inside path, keeping it much lower to the ground than the wristy action of Palmer and Casper. Charles's stroke is particularly slow and smooth – the key to this kind of stroke being 'low and slow'.

Jack Nicklaus

The unusual points about Nicklaus's method are the positions of his head and right arm. His eyes are directly over the ball, as one might expect, but his head is very much behind the ball, giving him a view of the putt along the line rather than above it. His right shoulder is held very low, with his weight apparently well towards the right foot, encouraging a low path to the backswing. Nicklaus's putting method uses a dominant right hand, with the right elbow out in a fairly acute angle and a virtual right angle formed between the back of the right hand and the forearm. The right hand works with a kind of pumping action from the elbow, the angle in the right wrist staying consistent, whereas for most of us it is consistency

For Jack it is the angle of the right elbow and wrist which seems to be the key rather than the left, a kind of 'pumping' action unique amongst the world's top players

Jack Nicklaus
with his very
distinctive style –
head back and
hands forward,
right shoulder
unusually low at
address to produce
the lowest and
smoothest of
backswings

in the left that is the aim. This trademark of the Nicklaus putting method stays the same from round to round, although he does by his own admission change other points from day to day and even from green to green. Sometimes he apparently sees the putter as moving from slightly open to closed and at other times from closed to open. Jack has probably holed more important putts than almost any other golfer, and although I could never see myself or most players putting from this right-shoulder-down, head-back position, it obviously has its merits. Perhaps the main points to learn from Jack are his methodical approach to each putt, his meticulous reading of greens and the exceptionally slow, rhythmic stroke.

Tom Watson

Tom's short-putting is probably the most aggressive in tournament golf. Like Gary Player, he rams the ball straight at the back of the hole on most short putts, minimizing the amount of break which is necessary to read into a putt. The firmer you hit a ball the less borrow you have to take, but this requires considerable confidence; you know that if the putt were to miss it would often run many feet past. Tom sets up with an orthodox reverse overlapping grip, thumbs on top of the shaft though not running straight down it, palms facing. He holds the left wrist high in an arched position with the hands pushed slightly ahead of the ball. He usually adopts a slightly open stance, his eyes, as with most good putters, seeming to be directly over the ball and his head in a roughly horizontal position. Tom's putting stroke is primarily an arm stroke, keeping the left wrist firm and the angle in the left wrist and elbow pretty constant throughout the stroke. Tom has a fairly fast, punchy kind of putting stroke, with a timing in clear contrast to the slow, smooth approach of Charles or Nicklaus. The main lessons from Tom's putting are the emphasis on the left elbow and wrist angle staying constant, combined with very marked aggressive short-putting, and the difference this can make to the reading of putts.

Opposite: Tom Watson, one of tournament golf's most aggressive putters. Tom sets his left wrist very high, elbow out, and then retains this solid unit with practically no wrist action except on the longest of putts

Ben Crenshaw, arms hanging straight yet very relaxed. Ben's stroke is so slow and smooth that he seems to swing the putter back and through much further than most players, naturally letting it come back on a shallow, curved path. Despite the looseness of his grip, the hands and wrists hardly seem to come into play

Ben Crenshaw

If most tournament professionals were asked who was the best long-putter on tour, they would be virtually unanimous in suggesting Ben. He has more feel for long putts and holes more of them than perhaps any other professional. He holds the club very lightly indeed, using a reverse overlap grip with both thumbs running absolutely straight down the front of the shaft. He plays the ball slightly forward in his stance with his hands slightly ahead of the ball, and then uses a very slow stroke, pivoting from the shoulders with no wrist action at all. The stroke is long and very smooth, travelling on a pronounced inside path on both backswing and through-swing. If anything he seems to strike the ball slightly on the upswing and

always sends it rolling beautifully smoothly. There are some players who immobilize the wrists for short-putting and use the hands and wrists far more with long-putting. Ben doesn't seem to do this and makes the stroke predominantly with the arms and shoulders, even with putts of considerable length. The particular points which are always so worth looking at in Ben's putting are the slowness and the very consistent rhythm. He never seems to hurry the putting stroke or to show any hitting action at the ball. Surprisingly for a player whom we think of as holing most long putts, he often describes his attitude as being one of just getting the ball very close – not what one would expect from one of the game's best long-putters.

Although Ben is primarily thought of by the rest of the pros as being an outstanding long-putter, he is also an excellent short-putter. Again, his stroke is longer than most players, very slow, and follows the same slightly inside arc for the backswing on short putts.

Another view of Ben, who makes long-putting look so very easy

Greg Norman showing the stance and stroke which took him to his first British Open in 1986 and so nearly won him the other three Majors of that year: an open stance, ball from the toe of the putter, but so simple and successful

5 Short-Putt Precision

My thoughts on short-putting and long-putting fall into two quite distinct categories. Short-putting to my mind is largely a question of a repetitive, well-rehearsed stroke, whereas long-putting is far more a question of good reading of the greens and feel and control for distance.

Having looked at some of the different schools of thought on putting and technique, can we really extract any common ground for building a putting stroke? If we go back to the principles of putting, we know that we are trying to set the clubface square at address and impact, that the putting stroke must be travelling in the right direction at impact, rolling the ball truly at the correct speed. All this has to be built into a repetitive stroke which withstands the pressure of competition. I believe we can find a considerable degree of common ground for developing a stroke.

- Square clubface
- Direction of impact
- Perfect roll from the sweet spot
- Speed and distance
- Repetitive stroke

Square Clubface

It is essential that the clubface is set squarely at address and returned squarely at impact. As a rule the easiest way of judging this square position and seeing the line of the putt is to have the eyes directly over the ball–target line. I suppose that most good putters naturally set the clubface square and have no particular problems in aiming it correctly. For some golfers setting the putter squarely in the first place is by no means easy. I know of several professional players who are constantly having to check the aim of the clubface and who find it difficult to set it at right angles to the line of the putt. Most of what I have read on putting or heard from

The square clubface is essential. Here I am at a tournament a few years ago, obviously trying to check it to the exact degree! Thankfully it usually happens quite naturally

other top golfers simply says that you set the putter squarely without saying how you go about it. **The square clubface is essential. To repeat, if your clubface is 1 degree out at impact it means the ball is $1\frac{1}{4}$ inches off line on a 6-foot putt.** That is a sufficient error to have the ball hitting the edge of the hole and spinning out.

Certain putters are easier to line up than others. A putter with a relatively long head may give you a better sense of a right angle than one with a neat, compact head. A putter face with virtually no loft can seem more difficult to square up than one with 4–5 degrees of loft. A putter with a fairly broad head from front to back with one or more lines at right angles to the clubface can make the task of achieving squareness easier. If you have any difficulty in setting the clubface squarely, it is well worth practising setting up against the corner of a sheet of card or paper to familiarize yourself with how the clubface looks when it is at right angles to the line of the putt.

It may help to have someone checking the putter face from behind when you practise. You will quite often see tournament professionals practising with their caddies squatting down close behind the putter to check the angle. A few years ago so many of the tournament professionals were having their caddies watching the putting stroke from this angle in tournament play that the rules had to be changed to stop it.

Head Position

Ideally the eyes should be directly over the ball to see the line from the ball to the target with the eyeline absolutely parallel to the putt. Theoretically from this position it is easiest to see the square clubface and the line of the putt. Almost all good putters also stand with their neck and head virtually horizontal in the set-up, whether or not they stand up well or crouch down to the putt. This enables the head to swivel back and forwards in looking along the line for a really accurate view, rather than the head lifting or turning. I would suggest that anyone trying to build a putting technique should aim first of all at adopting this position. In theory if your head is too far over the ball and your eyes outside the line of the putt there is a tendency to pull the ball to the left. I don't believe any great putter knowingly adopts this head position except possibly as a gimmick when trying to keep the ball left on a left-to-right putt. Seve Ballesteros says that he does this sometimes. Billy Casper is the only great putter I know of who stood so close to the ball that his eyes at times tended to get outside the line.

74

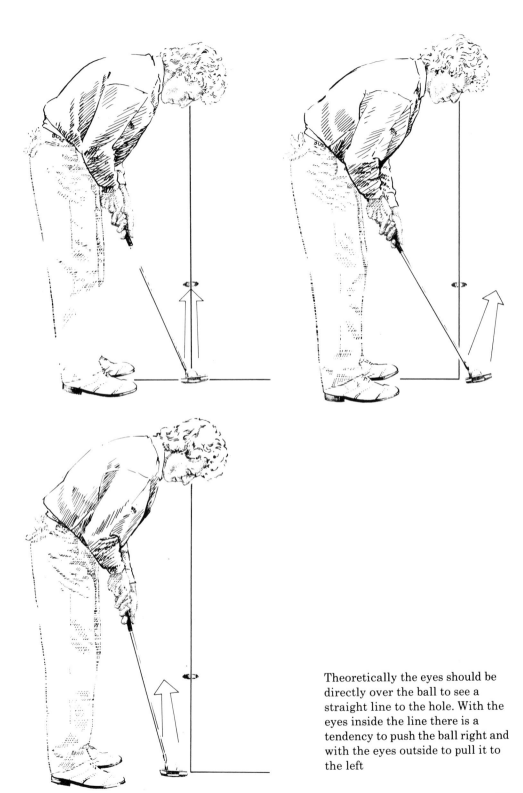

Theoretically the eyes should be
directly over the ball to see a
straight line to the hole. With the
eyes inside the line there is a
tendency to push the ball right and
with the eyes outside to pull it to
the left

75

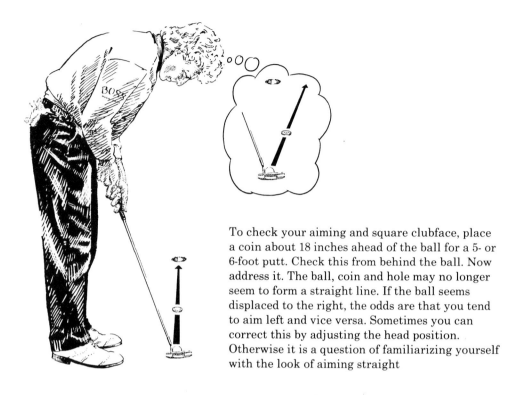

To check your aiming and square clubface, place a coin about 18 inches ahead of the ball for a 5- or 6-foot putt. Check this from behind the ball. Now address it. The ball, coin and hole may no longer seem to form a straight line. If the ball seems displaced to the right, the odds are that you tend to aim left and vice versa. Sometimes you can correct this by adjusting the head position. Otherwise it is a question of familiarizing yourself with the look of aiming straight

On the other hand, there are several good putters who have their eyes inside the line of the putt. I can only assume that they find it far easier to see the square clubface and judge the line to the ball from this position. Isao Aoki and Fuzzy Zoeller are the two who spring to mind most, Aoki's position being quite extreme. The view of a short putt from his set-up position must be quite different from mine. Instead of looking straight down on the line of the putt he obviously sees the ball and line to the hole out in front of him. The danger for anyone adopting this head position is that the clubhead is likely to move back and through in a far more curved path than when the eyes are directly over the line. It is much the same as in a full golf swing. The further you stand from the ball the more curved the attack, and the closer you stand the straighter the path.

I do, however, appreciate that the same head and eye position does not suit everyone and our vision of the putt obviously differs. It is essential that you see a good, clear straight line from the ball to the hole. A way of checking this is to place a small coin about 18 inches ahead of the ball directly between the ball and the hole for a 5–6 foot putt. Having lined this up from behind the ball you should hopefully find that the three objects – ball, coin and hole – still look in a straight line when you adopt your set-up position. For any really good putter, myself included, I don't believe there would ever be any difficulty in seeing the objects forming a straight line. For many who find putting difficult the coin will often no longer seem to be directly between the ball and the hole. I don't understand why it is, but if the coin seems to have moved to the right you probably tend to aim to the left and vice versa. Adjustment of the head position and ensuring that the eyes are parallel to the line are the first steps in trying to correct this and may be the reasons why some players need to set their eyes inside (or possibly even outside) the line of the putt.

The Grip

The grip in the long game largely controls the way in which the clubface is returned to the ball, whether square, open or closed. In putting it does much the same. In the long game players vary in the degree to which they have the left hand on top of the grip and the right one below it. Some players, like myself, have a relatively strong grip, with the left hand well on top, whereas others have a much weaker grip, with the palms virtually to the side of the club. In putting there is far less variation and you will find the top players, almost without exception, adopt a putting grip in which the palms face each other, with the back of the left hand and the palm of the right facing the hole. **The most standard putting grip to adopt is one in which both thumbs point straight down the front of the putter, *not* with the hands turned under and only the tips of the thumb on the front of the grip.** Your starting point should be to set both hands directly to the side of the club. If you use a conventional, right-hand-below-left grip, I would suggest you adopt a reverse overlap grip in which the left index finger either fits snugly around the little finger of the right hand or points virtually straight down partly covering the last three fingers of the right hand. There are variations on this grip, the most common of which is probably to push the right index finger slightly lower down the grip for extra control or even to have the tip of this finger at the back of the shaft, which may give a better feel. A putter with a flat-fronted grip encourages the kind of grip I have described.

I hope you are prepared to experiment with cross-handed putting. In principle a cross-handed grip should follow the same guidelines as a conventional grip, with the palms facing and the thumbs straight down the front of the grip. In my own grip I have seven fingers on the club, with the index finger of the right hand overlapping the little finger of my left hand. **The great merit of this is that my left arm can hang very relaxed and straight, with the left wrist straight, but I know that the wrist and arm won't break down through impact however light a grip I employ.**

My cross-handed grip from a different view

Left Arm and Wrist

It would obviously be wrong of me to suggest that the wristy methods of Arnold Palmer and Billy Casper are in any way incorrect, but for anyone in search of a putting technique I would certainly not suggest adopting a method in which the club is hinged backwards and forwards with the wrists. There is a fairly general consensus of opinion that the less wrist action you employ in the putting stroke the more reliable it is likely to be. Both Palmer and Casper acknowledge that their method required an extraordinary amount of work to perfect it and I would suggest that it also required exceptional talent to use it effectively. Therefore we should look at methods which reduce the wrist action and in particular which do not allow the left wrist and arm to collapse and break down through and beyond impact.

There are different ways in which you can set about trying to achieve this. Some players, like Andy North, Ben Crenshaw and Craig Stadler, hang both arms relatively straight at address so that the left wrist and elbow are set to the ball with very little bending in the first place. Other players, like Tom Watson and Seve Ballesteros, show a far more pronounced angle in the left elbow and the left wrist at address but then work at maintaining this angle throughout the stroke. An extreme way of achieving this was the style of Leo Diegel in the 1930s. He set his left elbow in a sharply acute angle, pointing it out towards the target and locking it like this throughout the stroke. Not something to copy but worth being aware of.

To my mind any good short-putting stroke must work at this principle of keeping the left arm and left wrist constant through impact to keep the putter head square and the club travelling on line. There are two stumbling blocks to this. The first is that, for most of us, good putting requires both a relaxed attitude of mind and also physical relaxation. It is one of the points stressed time and again by the good putters, again going back to Bobby Locke and his idea of holding the putter very loosely, or in modern times Ben Crenshaw and his very loose grip. How do you combine relaxation and a light sensitive touch with a left arm and wrist which does not break down through impact? The second point is that with a conventional grip, right hand below left, there is a tendency to shorten the left arm at address to enable the right hand to grip below the other. In the long game this problem is overcome by a good golfer dropping the right shoulder noticeably below the left to keep the left arm straight at address. In putting the same thing follows. There are only two ways of keeping the left arm

Above: Tom Watson, with a pronounced angle in the left wrist and elbow, but firmly maintained through and beyond impact

Opposite: My cross-handed putting stroke, with the left wrist straight but relaxed and without any fear of it buckling through impact. At address the weight of the putter is supported by my arms, not resting on the ground. This encourages a smooth takeaway. The head is horizontal and my putter travels straight back and through, putter face looking at the target throughout, and with a slight under-and-up movement. Interestingly the camera has caught me just beyond the moment of impact with the ball airborne

80

and wrist straight at address and through impact. The first is to allow the right shoulder to drop quite markedly at address to bring the right hand below the left. The second is to adopt the cross-handed grip with the left arm hanging straight, the left hand below the right and the right arm becoming the one which folds and tucks in. Very few professional players adopt a method in which the left arm hangs truly straight. Even Craig Stadler and Ben Crenshaw show some angle in the left elbow.

This is where I believe the benefits of cross-handed putting can be enormous. The left arm in hanging naturally straight can be very relaxed and yet without the fear of the left elbow and wrist buckling through impact. With an orthodox grip I often felt that the left wrist and elbow had to be bent at address to get myself into a comfortable position. From this position I felt that I would become too tense in the stroke or alternatively it allowed me to yip the putt, with the right hand taking over and the left one breaking down through impact.

The Address Position

Amongst good putters the address position can vary enormously. As we have already seen, there are so many contrasting styles that one must almost say that anything goes. But this is not helpful if you are in search of a putting technique or find yourself with severe putting troubles, as I did. Again, it would be wrong for me to say that Aoki's putting or Palmer's putting or Nicklaus's putting is wrong just because I don't adopt their methods. What I think we must do is look at several styles of set-up so that we can judge what suits us best. We can see what kind of stroke each set-up is likely to produce.

I am going to start by looking at a set-up like Ben Crenshaw's. As I have already said, Ben sets up with both arms hanging relatively straight, the right shoulder slightly lower than the left. To achieve this he stands fairly upright but with his head just above a horizontal position, eyes directly over the line of the putt or if anything fractionally inside. The ball is kept opposite his left heel, hands slightly ahead of the ball at address and indeed through the whole stroke. From this kind of set-up the swing feels like a pendulum stroke, arms and wrists staying as a unit and the shoulders pivoting as though from a point at the back of the neck.

If we look next at the style Seve Ballesteros uses we see a different technique. Seve bends over considerably more, probably feeling more comfortable and able to see the putts better with his head held relatively low. The back of his head is roughly horizontal, enabling him to swivel it back and forwards as he looks along the line of the putt. By getting over the ball in this way one of two things will follow. Either the arms will be quite bent – as we see in Seve's position – or the player will need to adopt an address position like Andy North's in which both arms hang straight and grip the club perhaps only 18 inches from the ground. But, without going to these extremes, any player who uses a relatively crouched position is going to find that the arms bend more, and this, to my mind, can easily be a source of trouble for both club player and professional alike. In Seve's case the left arm shows quite an angle at address, with the back of the left wrist fairly bent. What is noticeable is that Seve also keeps the right shoulder relatively low at address, not as extreme as Nicklaus or Johnny Miller, but rather in the same mould, with the right elbow and right wrist quite bent. The lower the right shoulder is kept at address the easier it is to keep the putter head swinging low to the ground on the backswing. From this position Seve can strike the ball at the very bottom of the stroke or perhaps even slightly on the upswing.

Seve Ballesteros, from a low right shoulder position at address, left elbow very bent, giving a shallow backswing and upward attack on the ball

Any player who adopts an address position like Seve's, with the arms relatively bent, but without keeping the right shoulder low, would probably find the putter head rising, perhaps unsuitably, in the backswing.

Thirdly, there is my own putting stance. I hope that readers of this book will give cross-handed putting a try. Obviously I believe in it myself or I wouldn't use it. But I also believe many golfers would find it has real

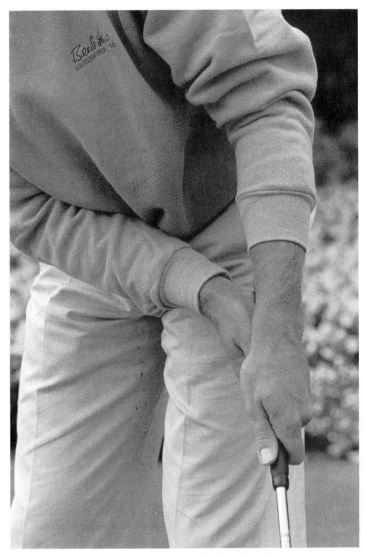

Another view of my cross-handed grip showing the constant, unbroken unit of hand and wrist through impact

benefits if they would only persevere with the slightly awkward initial feeling. My own set-up overcomes what to me is the greatest problem with short-putting and that is one of keeping the left arm and wrist as a solid unit throughout the stroke. As I set up to the ball my left arm hangs naturally in a straight position, the right one is tucked in, and the right shoulder stays back although the shoulders remain fairly horizontal.

As a general principle I would suggest that the club golfer is best advised to adopt a position in which he stands up as much as possible at address, giving maximum chance of having both arms hanging relatively straight, while at the same time with the head over in an almost horizontal position.

Direction and Ball Position

I favour a square stance for short-putting and would suggest that this should be the starting point for building a good, solid technique. Having set the clubface to the hole, follow this line with the feet and indeed with the whole body right up to the shoulders. The squarer you can be with the clubface and body, the easier it should theoretically be to keep the putter travelling on line through impact. Obviously there are players who do not use a perfectly square stance. Tom Watson and Ben Crenshaw both seem to adopt a slightly open stance, Hubert Green and Greg Norman at times use an extremely open one, and Bobby Locke used a very closed one. So, again, we cannot say that it has to be a square stance. I would, however, suggest that a perfectly square stance should be considered the norm and that you should only experiment with this if it clearly is not working for you. If you do feel you need to adjust the stance to a slightly open or closed one, then I would suggest that the line of the shoulders should still be square at address and not necessarily follow the line of your feet. As with the long game, there is a pronounced tendency for most golfers to pull the right shoulder forward in getting the right hand below the left on the grip. Again, this is a problem which a cross-handed grip overcomes for now it becomes quite easy to keep the right shoulder back in a square or even fractionally closed position.

An ideal ball position to adopt is one in which the ball is just opposite the inside of the left heel. Most players will find that this naturally produces a stroke in which the putter head strikes the ball at the very bottom of the swing or fractionally on the upswing. Again, much the same principles follow as in the long game. The farther back you play the ball

in your stance, the more likely you are to hit it slightly on the downswing. If you see the putter head as moving on a very slightly curved arc you can also see that the farther back you have the ball in the stance the more likely you are to hit the ball before it reaches the straight through part of the arc and therefore, if anything, to push it away to the right. Conversely if you play the ball too far forward there is a likelihood of hitting it too much on the upswing and of catching it beyond the straight through part of the arc, tending to pull it to the left. Perhaps golfers who play on relatively poor greens are more likely to adopt a stroke with the ball back in the feet and a slightly downward attack. Professionals who putt for the most part on good surfaces are more likely to play the ball well forward and see the putting stroke as one in which the ball is rolled smoothly with a flat or slightly upward stroke.

With the ball in this standard position opposite the left instep, it should mean that the shaft of the putter will naturally sit straight up towards you, with the hands, if anything, fractionally ahead of the putter. If your hands lag behind the ball at address, the left wrist is already showing signs of weakness and the right hand is likely to take over unsatisfactorily through impact, tending to close the clubface. On the other hand it is equally a mistake to push the hands too far forward at address. This tends to reduce the loft of the club, possibly even turning it into a negative loft position, and also to produce too much of a downward attack, often leaving the putter blade open at impact. In a good, standard set-up the hands should be fractionally ahead of the ball without tipping the shaft forward from its natural position.

The Putting Stroke

There is no doubt that professionals do not agree on the nature of the putting stroke and I think we must accept that there are several different kinds of stroke. The main question is whether you see the putting stroke for short distances, say up to 6 feet, as being straight back and through on a line, or whether you see it as being on a slightly curved path. A routine which is frequently used is to swing the putter back and through on a straight line between two club shafts lying on the ground to groove

Opposite: Greg Norman with a particularly open stance, showing that you don't have to stand square at address. To me squareness is essential; to others it isn't

I, and most other tournament professionals, like to feel that the stroke for a short putt is perfectly straight-back-and-through. In reality, if you adopt a true pendulum stroke from the centre of the shoulders, the putter head probably does describe a very slightly curved arc

a good stroke. This is certainly my own feeling for a short putt but it is by no means unanimously accepted.

It is worth looking at the mechanics of the putting stroke to see exactly what in theory should happen. If you use a pendulum stroke from the shoulders, the centre of that stroke is a point in about the middle of your neck, and with your eyes positioned directly over the ball this point is likely to be 6–8 inches inside the line from ball to target. A true pendulum stroke from this point would therefore bring the putter slightly inside the line of the putt as it rises in the backswing and rises again in the throughswing. Putters are designed so that the hands cannot be directly above the ball when the putter head is sitting flat on the ground. The rules provide that the club shaft must sit at an angle of at least 10 degrees to the vertical. In theory if you could have the hands directly above the ball the putter head could be swung backwards and forwards on a straight line with a pendulum stroke centred on the top of the putter and the hands. Everything therefore suggests that, if we adopt a simple pendulum stroke, the putter head must in reality describe a slightly curved path when looked at from above.

But in a putting stroke and a golf swing what actually happens and what we feel has to happen are by no means always the same thing. For a short putt some players, myself included, like to *feel* that the putter head travels back and through on a perfectly straight line. My feeling is that the putter head travels straight back a few inches with the putter head square to this line and the putter face looking slightly downwards. Then, as I swing through, I feel it again travels in a straight line, the putter face looking upwards quite naturally beyond the ball. This is certainly what I *feel* happens, although in reality the putter head probably does move fractionally inside the line on both backswing and throughswing. Certainly I accept that, once I have a putt of more than 6 feet or so (depending on the speed), the putter head must be moving fractionally inside the line. **A straight line approach to short-putting has certain merits. In particular the ball position is relatively unimportant and it should not really matter whether you catch the ball fractionally on the downswing, at the bottom of the swing or fractionally on the upswing. At each stage the putter is moving in the correct direction and the putter face is square to the hole.** I believe that anyone looking for a good, sound short-putting stroke should adopt this straight-line feeling. But why is it right for some golfers and not for others?

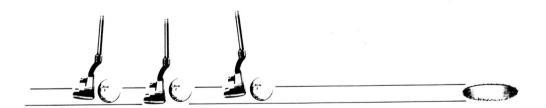

One of the advantages of a straight-back-and-through stroke is that the putter face looks at the target from start to finish. The exact ball position and point in the stroke at which the ball is struck is flexible within reason. If you use a curved arc by contrast and strike the ball fractionally earlier or later in the stroke, you can set the ball off on the wrong line

Using an upright putter and high
hand and wrist position
encourages a straight path to the
stroke. A low position produces
far more of a curve

In order to produce the feeling of a straight-line approach to short-putting two things are essential if you are going to use a wrist-free pendulum stroke. **First, you should use a putter whose shaft sits upright, so that your hands, and in particular your left hand, are held fairly high. The higher your hands at address the more naturally the putter head should move back and through in a straight line.** The lower your hands at address, and the more pronounced the angle between left hand and wrist, the more curved an arc you are likely to produce. **Secondly, your putter head path will more naturally follow a straight line if you keep your head and neck well over the ball in a horizontal position,** even though you should probably aim for a fairly upright address position. If you hold your head in this position your shoulders are more likely to rotate quite naturally in a fairly vertical path, producing a straight line. The higher you hold your neck and head the more likely your shoulders are to turn at an angle to the vertical, with the putter head feeling it wants to describe a curved path. Ben Crenshaw shows a little of this head position, producing a curved path for short and long putts.

I therefore believe that the starting point for a good short-putting technique is to adopt an address position which encourages this straight-back-and-through path. What is damaging is that a lot of players work at swinging the putter head back and through in a straight line without adopting an address position which is conducive to doing this. If you adopt a set-up in which you crouch well over, bend both arms quite markedly, hold the hands quite low at address and use a putter which sits relatively flat, I do not believe the putter head will naturally follow a straight path. It will only do so with a series of compensatory movements. If you adopt this address position and try to swing the putter straight back and straight through, you will almost certainly have to turn the wrists underneath on the backswing, almost hooding the clubface and forcing the arms out away from the body to take the putter straight back. You will then have to compensate for this and make a slightly unnatural movement in the throughswing. If you feel you can only putt from this position, possibly if you are a very tall player for whom crouching over is the only way, then you will have to see your putting stroke as following more of a curved path. If you see short-putting as requiring a curved path, you should bear in mind that, as the putter head moves slightly inside on the backswing, the clubface stays square to *this path* and so turns off the line of the putt. It must then strike the ball at exactly the right point in the stroke and return slightly inside on the throughswing. If you catch the ball early there is a tendency to meet it with swing and clubface out to the right; if you meet it slightly late there is a tendency to meet it with swing and clubface slightly left. Personally I feel this kind of stroke is far more difficult to perfect than the straight-back-and-through approach. But this must depend on how comfortable you feel at address and whether you are able to stand up tall or need to crouch down low.

The Strike

We have dealt with the first two principles of short-putting – the clubface and direction. We now need to work on rolling the ball smoothly.

You must decide how you are trying to strike the ball. Do you want to hit it on the downswing, at the bottom of the swing or on the upswing? If you adopt a pendulum-type stroke, with the putter head moving back and through in a straight line, the putter head will naturally rise and fall and rise again in a kind of saucer-shaped arc. The putter stroke and clubface are on target all the time, and from a directional point of view it should not matter where in the stroke the ball is struck. You want to get it rolling properly, and in order to do this the putter head should strike the ball at a consistent depth. Obviously you must not brush the ground at impact, but you need to get virtually to the bottom of the ball, in my view either striking it right at the bottom of the swing or slightly on the upswing. It is widely suggested that if you hit the ball on the upswing you will actually impart top spin and keep the ball rolling more accurately. However, a physicist would probably say that this isn't what happens at all. But certainly that is what a lot of professional golfers feel can be achieved by striking the ball fractionally on the upswing. If, on the other hand, you see the putting stroke as a curved path, then you should try to make contact at the very bottom of the stroke. The odds are that, if you catch it slightly on the upswing, the stroke and the clubhead will by this time be aimed slightly left and the putt may be pulled. If you feel there are merits in striking the ball slightly on the upswing, then with a conventional grip and stance you can adopt an address position in which the right shoulder is held fairly low. Now the putter head is more likely to swing low on the backswing and up on the throughswing. Again, you have to see any pieces of golfing advice in the context of your own set-up. A common piece of advice is to keep the putter low on the backswing. If you want to try that, it is possible with this sort of set-up. If, on the other hand, you have latched onto advice to keep the putter head low beyond impact, you will find it is quite incompatible with a low right shoulder at address.

My own opinion, and the starting point I would advocate, is that you should develop a simple pendulum stroke from the shoulders, with the putter head naturally rising and falling in a symmetrical arc, and not work at keeping it particularly low going back or going through.

The Last 6 Inches

Judgement of distance with short-putting is far less difficult than it is with long-putting. But that does not mean it is unimportant. Good putters vary in their approach to short-putting. Some players like the idea of the ball rolling relatively slowly as it approaches the hole, feeling that there is more chance for a ball running fairly slowly to drop in from the side of the hole. Others, like Tom Watson and Gary Player, adopt a far more aggressive approach, running the ball hard at the back of the hole. Broadly speaking, the firmer you are with each putt the straighter you can afford to hit it for it will take less break. If you aim at trickling the ball into the edge of the hole, it will take the maximum possible borrow with the contours of the ground and your reading must be precise. The slower the greens the easier it is to get away with a poor putting stroke. There are not many players with Tom's courage to attack the ball on fast greens. But a lot of golfers, both amateur and professional, are at times too cautious with their short putts, hitting them too gently to hold a good line.

It is important to understand how a ball reacts in the last 6 inches or so of its path. As the ball slows to a stop it reacts far more to the slope and to any little irregularities than it does over the rest of the putt. All too often a ball seems on line to drop and may then surprisingly pull up short, swerve off line or curve away alarmingly with the slope of the ground. The last 6 inches are vital, with the ball reacting quite severely at this stage. For this reason a ball which is dying at the hole needs to be read perfectly to allow for any borrow. It also needs a perfect surface to run predictably. Often a hole will become slightly crowned, with the area 3–4 inches from the hole being trodden down throughout the day. A ball travelling too slowly can easily reach this point and then, to the surprise and dismay of the player, break off line.

The lesson to learn from this is to ensure that the ball will travel at least 6 inches past the hole to avoid the crucial 6-inch zone taking effect. To be on the safe side, whether the green is fast or slow, I believe you should aim at stopping the ball about 15 inches beyond the hole. This gives it a good chance of holding the line without the

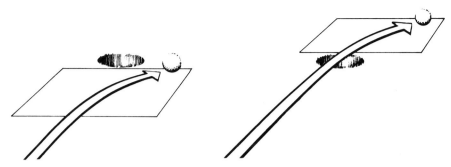

The last 6 inches of the natural roll of a putt is the danger or 'wobble' zone, where the ball is slowing down and is influenced by any little irregularities on the green or any crowning to the hole. On a perfect, newly cut green the ball may hold its line if you 'die' it into the hole. But so often a ball which isn't hit quite firmly enough approaches the hole as though going to drop and then wobbles off line. Aim at hitting your putts firmly enough to put this wobble zone beyond the hole and critically assess those which do miss to see if the strength was at fault.

danger of running too far past. In grooving your stroke you should look critically at the length of the putts which miss to see whether you are producing this kind of distance.

Length of Stroke

There are obviously different ideas about how you strike the ball. Ben Crenshaw has a fairly long, smooth stroke even for relatively short putts, whereas other players like to use a short, firm type of tapping stroke. If you use a long, flowing stroke there is a danger of falling into the trap of slowing down through impact. If you slow down through impact, just as with full golf shots, you usually lose the line. It is all too common to see poor putters taking an overlong backswing and then decelerating. But at the other end of the scale I don't believe it is right to encourage a very short, tapping stroke. For anyone but the very good putter this is all too likely to cause a quick, jerky stroke which is unlikely to stand up to tournament pressure. Whatever the type of stroke, aim at a fairly symmetrical path, back and through.

The starting point is to adopt a smooth stroke which feels fairly slow, but not awkwardly slow, but without the feeling of a definite hit or acceleration on the ball. Just say to yourself 'One-two' or 'Back and through'. Try to give yourself a steady rhythm. The length of the putting stroke should then quite naturally control the length of the putt.

Keeping Still for Reliability

As we have seen, there are so many ways in which you can putt that it is hard to say which is right or wrong. What is essential is that you decide on a putting stroke, practise religiously to make it repetitive, and then stick with it. Many people experience problems with short-putting because they read so much conflicting advice that they are forever experimenting with one thing or another without really grooving a stroke and giving it a chance to work. I hope you will have decided to adopt a stroke with a predominantly straight-back-and-through feeling. Having decided on this, it is necessary to practise the stroke time and again until you can repeat it flawlessly.

To help you develop a good stroke, work at keeping the body, and in particular the head, perfectly still from start to finish without getting tense. It is all too easy in your anxiety to look at the hole to lift your head early, bringing the putter off line just before the ball is struck. Practise grooving the stroke without the ball initially, swinging the putter head back and through and actually making yourself watch it to check its path and squareness. Once you have the ball in front of you, your eyes should be focused on a specific spot on the back of the ball until the moment of impact, and should then stay focused on this same area, as if on an after-image of the ball, until it is well on its way. The difficulty in grooving a stroke is that you should keep your head still, and yet at the same time you want to see the ball to analyse its success or failure and, in practice at least, to check the end of the putting stroke to see where the putter has finished.

Take time to test your peripheral vision to the left without moving the eyes. You probably have quite clear vision for a 3–4 foot putt without any eye movement. With putts of up to 6 feet or so make quite certain that if you do watch the ball as it reaches the hole you swivel only your eyes rather than your head. If you stand up well at address you can probably do this for a longer putt than if you crouch down excessively. My advice to anyone developing a putting technique is to try to keep the head as still as possible and to be aware of listening for the ball to drop in the hole rather than watching it. **Without doubt the most widely accepted advice on putting technique is that more putts are ruined by moving the head and body prematurely than by anything else.**

We have looked at the first four principles of precision putting – the clubface, the stroke, a perfect roll and good distance. By now you should have decided on your method and it is time to make that putting stroke work on the course. This comes from sound reading of the greens, constructive practice and an understanding of the strategy and mental aspects of the game.

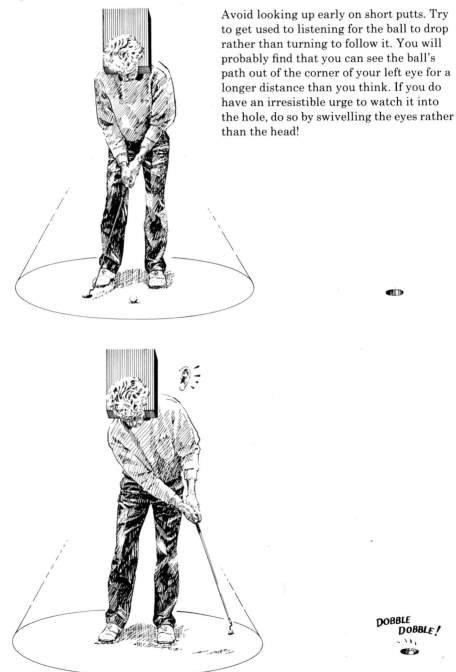

Avoid looking up early on short putts. Try to get used to listening for the ball to drop rather than turning to follow it. You will probably find that you can see the ball's path out of the corner of your left eye for a longer distance than you think. If you do have an irresistible urge to watch it into the hole, do so by swivelling the eyes rather than the head!

DOBBLE DOBBLE!

6 Selecting a Putter

Just as there are many ways of putting, there are numerous types of putter on the market. It is difficult to say what is the right putter for any individual because in the end it comes down to personal preference and confidence. I do, however, think it is important that you realize the merits of the different styles of putter.

The Sweet Spot

A point which always concerns me first in choosing a putter is the sweet spot, i.e. the optimum hitting area. One of our key points for good putting is to ensure that the clubface is always returned squarely to the ball. To keep the clubface square through impact the ball needs to be struck from just the right point, the sweet spot. This is the point from which you will get the most solid hit and about which, in effect, the clubface is balanced. If you strike the ball correctly with this spot the clubface stays square. If you strike the ball nearer the heel or the toe, then the clubface is likely to turn and send the ball off line, to left or right respectively. In recent years putter designers have been aiming at producing a relatively large sweet spot on the putter head so that the exact point of striking the ball is less critical.

To find the sweet spot on a putter, the easiest way is to hang the putter loosely by holding it between the thumb and index finger of your left hand with the putter head towards you, and then tap the face of the club with a tee or the tip or nail of your right index finger along the length of its face. If you start by tapping at the toe end of the putter you will probably feel the putter vibrating in your left hand and will be aware that the putter face is wanting to turn. As you approach the centre of the putter head you will feel it beginning to move straight backwards and forwards rather than twisting, and the vibration felt in the left hand is reduced. As you get farther along towards the heel of the club you can again feel that the

putter head wants to twist and again the vibration felt in the left hand increases. The point on the putter face at which you feel the least vibration in the left hand, and at which the putter head seems to move straight back rather than twisting, is the sweet spot.

With any putter, it is important to locate this point and mark it, possibly at first simply with a pencil or ink mark. **Ideally, particularly if you are not a naturally good putter, you want a putter with a relatively long sweet spot. By tapping along the putter face in this way and comparing several putters you will find that the sweet spot on some putters is much larger than on others.** On an old-fashioned blade putter or on any putter where the shaft is attached to the head directly at the heel, the sweet spot may be relatively small. You may in effect only have at the most a quarter of an inch to play with. Hit the ball slightly towards the toe, and the ball will almost certainly be deflected to the right; hit it towards the heel, and the chances are it will go off to the left. It is useful to compare this with the sweet spot on one of the centre-shafted putters, such as the Acushnet Bullseye or the Golden Goose, whose shaft is attached to the head probably a third of the way along. The sweet spot of these putters is usually fairly near the bottom of the shaft and you will probably find there is an area perhaps half an inch long which gives a good solid strike.

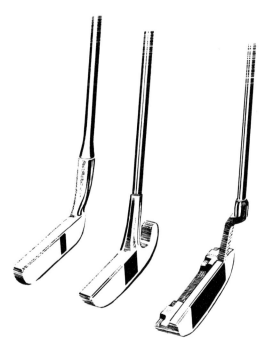

Right: Some putters are designed to give much larger sweet spots than others. Generally a blade putter has a relatively narrow spot giving a perfect strike; a centre-shafted putter increases the area; and the heel and toe type of style developed by Ping broadens it even further to give a large hitting zone from which no twist is felt

Opposite: Tapping the face of a putter to feel the sweet spot – the point where there is minimum turn or twist

99

In recent years the Ping putter design has aimed at concentrating the weight in the putter head towards the toe and the heel with the idea of substantially increasing the area for a solid strike, so that finding the exact sweet spot becomes far less important. If you try the same face-tapping experiment with one of these putters you will probably find there is much less twisting to the clubhead and vibration through the club shaft over quite a sizeable area around the middle of the clubhead.

One of the main aims with a good short-putting stroke must be to strike the ball accurately from the sweet spot. There is no doubt that some putters are much more sympathetic than others to a slight error. I would suggest that all but the very finest putters lack true accuracy in striking the ball with the right spot. Most club golfers are probably far less accurate in this than they imagine. It is worthwhile experimenting with any putter which may look attractive before you contemplate buying it. Having purchased a new putter, find the sweet spot, mark it temporarily in pencil, then experiment with the putter, and if you are certain that you have found the right spot, make a permanent mark on the top or back of the head to show exactly where you want to strike the ball. A manufacturer sometimes will mark a line on the putter which he assumes to be the sweet spot but which in fact is not accurate. Such a line may be useful in actually helping you to good alignment, but it may mislead you into hitting the ball with the wrong part of the clubface. If at some stage you change the lie of your putter, i.e. the angle between the head and the shaft, this can marginally alter the position of the sweet spot, so that it may need reassessing and remarking.

Length and Lie

It is vital to get the right lie, that is, the right shaft angle for your own particular height and method, and also to get the right length of putter. Putters vary quite markedly in the angle of the shaft. The most upright putter allowed under the rules is one in which there is a 10-degree angle between the shaft and the vertical when the putter head is flat to the ground. It is certainly unusual to find a manufacturer making a putter as upright as this. To a certain extent the more upright a putter you use, providing the clubhead sits flat, the more likely you are to swing the putter head back and through on a straight line with your short-putting stroke. If, on the other hand, you use a putter with a flat lie, your hands will obviously have to be dropped far lower at address, giving a substantial angle between the arms and the putter shaft, and making it more likely that you will swing the putter back and through in a relatively curved arc. The choice of the lie of a putter is crucial. It should not be a question of finding a new putter and then adapting your method to it, but rather ensuring that you select a putter which has the right lie for your putting stroke.

The lie of a putter can very often be altered, though this depends on the construction of the head and neck of the putter and the kind of metal used. Most metals will bend quite easily; some metals, however, are brittle and tend to snap. It is always well worth asking the professional who sells you a putter whether it can be altered if the mood takes you.

I would suggest also looking at the sole of the putter. Ideally you want a putter which sits flat on the ground. Obviously there are some players who tend to putt with the toe off the ground, Aoki being the prime example of this, but any player who does this may experience the heel of the putter dragging along the ground through impact, with a tendency to twist the putter face closed at the moment of impact. It is, therefore, a potentially dangerous method to adopt. What you should realize, however, is that you will not always be putting on a perfectly horizontal surface, so the lie of a putter needs to be reasonably adaptable in setting up on sideslopes. Much the same arises in miniature in putting as it does in the long game. If you stand above the ball, the tendency is to bring the ball closer to your feet and the putter shaft will sit more upright; if you are standing below the ball you are likely to push the putter farther from your feet with your hands lower. The effect can be substantial with long-game sideslopes and relatively minor in putting. But it is worth considering, and for this reason I always like a putter with a very slightly curved sole. You will usually find that most really well-designed putters have a very slight curve, and a head shaped like this is certainly more sympathetic to slightly sloping lies and a change in your method than a putter head with a perfectly flat sole.

At the same time as looking at the lie of a putter it is necessary to consider the length. If you have an upright putter which is fairly short you are more likely to be able to hang the left arm straight quite naturally while holding the shaft towards the top of the grip. If you feel that you want a putter with a flat lie your hands will obviously be lower at address and the putter shaft may need to be longer. It is, however, a mistake in my view to use a putter which is unsuitably long, particularly with a fairly upright lie, for it tends to encourage players to bend the left arm, or indeed both arms, unsuitably in trying to grip near the top of the club. The general range of putter lengths made by most manufacturers is between 33 and 36 inches. A 35-inch putter is probably a fairly good starting point, with the possibility of having it cut down and regripped should the need arise.

Loft and Shaft

There has been quite a lot written over the years concerning the ideal loft for a putter. Bobby Jones's famous putter, nicknamed 'Calamity Jane', apparently had 8 degrees of loft. By modern standards that is considerable and most putters now are manufactured with loft in the range of 2–5 degrees. The loft on a putter is worth considering. Obviously professionals like myself have access to good equipment and can easily measure loft. If you are an amateur golfer you may not be able to test a putter's loft to the exact degree, but you can at least look at it quite carefully. My own preference is for a putter with about 3–4 degrees of loft on fast greens, moving up to one with 5–6 degrees if I find myself putting on rough or fairly slow greens. My reasons for increasing the loft on bad greens are twofold. First of all, it gives you room to push the hands slightly forward

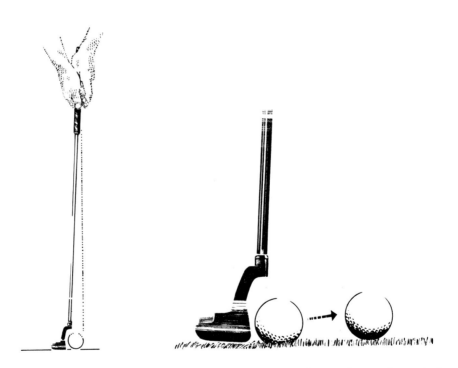

If the greens are at all slow or rough I like to use a putter of 5 to 6 degrees instead of my usual 3 to 4. I push the hands forward a little for a firmer stroke, and whenever the hands are in this position some loft is needed to avoid a negative angle to the face

102

at address without risking delofting the putter. This can be helpful in striking the ball more firmly and with a little more authority. Secondly, I also have the feeling that if you increase the loft very slightly on a bad green it is easier to set the ball rolling on its way smoothly on top of the grass. With insufficient loft it is easy to get caught up within the first few inches of the putt, pushing the ball into the ground and making it bounce unsatisfactorily. The exact loft of a putter is in some ways not very crucial. You would probably have to move up to a loft of about 9 degrees before actually seeing the ball get fractionally airborne.

However, there is a danger in using a putter which has too little loft or even a negative loft, as this makes it difficult to produce a smooth roll. Any player who putts with the hands pushed forward towards the left at address and through impact is certainly going to need a putter with some loft. If, on the other hand, you choose a putter which has a wry neck, then this may well push your hands forward quite naturally without delofting the putter head. It is worth noting that it is sometimes easier to have the feeling of lining up a putter accurately if you can see the clubface itself because of its loft, rather than simply looking down on the top of the clubhead.

The loft of a putter can often be altered in just the same way as the lie of a putter can be altered. This should only be done by an experienced club repairer. Adding loft can sometimes make the putter seem to sit in an unnaturally closed position. The back of the sole may no longer sit flat to the ground and may need skilled adjustment.

It is well worth experimenting with different kinds of shafts. Many tournament professionals use a very stiff shaft, giving the feeling of a nice, solid hit without the ball springing off too fast. For professionals putting on fast tournament greens the stiff shaft often seems to give more control. For a club golfer I would suggest that a stiff shaft is right for the sort of player who uses a fairly short, firm type of stroke. If, on the other hand, you use a fairly soft shaft you may find that it gives you better feeling, particularly on long putts, but perhaps with a tendency for the ball to come off more quickly for the short putt. My own preference is certainly for a fairly soft shaft, but just stiff enough to get a solid contact with plenty of control for short putts. Few professionals now use hickory shafts because of the problems encountered when moving from one climate to another. A hickory shaft can, however, give a really nice sense of feel, particularly on long putts, even though personally I feel they lack sufficient control for both short and long putts.

Putting Grips and Alignment

Ten or twenty years ago you would have found most professional golfers putting with a putter with a standard round or almost round grip. **Now it is fairly generally accepted that the easiest type of putting grip is one in which the front of the grip is flat**. There are still players who use conventional, round grips, but for most of us the flat-fronted grip has benefits. Your thumbs feel naturally comfortable at the front/top of the grip, rather than at the side, and this in turn should correctly place your hands to the side of the putter, with the back of the left hand and the palm of the right hand facing the hole. This kind of putter grip as we have discussed before gives maximum chance of returning the clubface squarely to the ball.

Most of the unusual putter designs on the market seem to be aimed at giving the player the best possible chance of lining up the clubface with the hole and also producing a straight-back-and-through path with the short-putting stroke. A fairly broad-headed putter with one, two or more lines at right angles to the putter face can help you see a right angle and set the putter face squarely. Being aware of these lines on the putter, without actually focusing on them in the backswing, will perhaps also make it easier for you to see that the putter head moves straight back and through. You will soon become aware of a suspect path and can set about

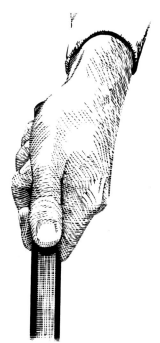

Most professionals now use putters with flat-fronted grips. This helps to put the thumbs down the front of the grip, with the palms directly facing and on target

104

correcting it. However, the actual feel of the putter and the suitability of its sweet spot, lie and length are really more important than the design. The design of a putter might certainly make me interested in using it, but I would have to be satisfied on various other points before simply falling for something unusual. If you choose a putter with some sort of flange or fairly broad head but without any markings there is no reason why you should not experiment with your own markings on the putter in some temporary form and if you then find them of use make some permanent mark for guidance.

Putter Weight

Standard putters probably vary in weight from about 15 to 18 oz. There are one or two on the market which as a special feature are much heavier than this, but most professional golfers use a putter which is around 17 oz. If you use a putter which is particularly light I always feel that it means that you have to put in too much effort to get the ball moving and are probably likely to develop a jerky stroke. My own preference is for a heavy putter which I feel helps produce a nice, slow stroke without any feeling of having to hit the ball firmly. The balance of a putter is difficult to describe, and it is difficult to tell someone else how to pick up a putter and know whether it feels right. I like to feel the weight very much in the clubhead so that I get an impression of the shaft and grip being relatively light and of the head being fairly heavy. This 'head-heavy' feeling encourages the slow, pendulum kind of stroke. A lot of professionals also recommend using a heavy putter on slow greens and a light one on fast greens. I do not necessarily go along with this; for most of us a heavy putter can be effective on any type of green and we can move on to a very heavy putter for slow greens. A light putter often produces a jerky action in many players and does not encourage a pendulum type of rhythm.

Selecting a putter is an individual choice. My starting point for someone who has no set ideas about putters would be to select a standard centre-shafted putter or to look for one of the heel–toe putters of a fairly conventional design. Some players suggest that you should choose a putter and then stick to it through thick and thin. Others believe that the best way to recover lost form is to change your putter and hope it inspires confidence. Having suffered bad times in the past, I love to experiment with different putters and I must admit to having a collection of about seventy. I do not by any means use all of them in tournament play, but I suppose I am always in search of the perfect putter which will never fail!

7 Long-Putting Technique

Short-putting is very much a question of producing a good stroke and practising it until it is completely repetitive even under pressure. Although the stroke for longer putts must show a reasonable degree of precision, the skill is far more a matter of reading the greens well, making a good assessment and having feel for the distance, and then developing 'touch' for setting the ball rolling with just the right speed. It would be wrong to suggest that the stroke is of no consequence at all. Many amateurs I play with in pro-ams come unstuck with long putts through striking the ball inaccurately, either sending it off on quite a different line from the one chosen, or striking it poorly and leaving the ball short. But on the whole for long putts a player can be far less concerned with the stroke and can concentrate on developing a good eye for reading greens and a feel for distance.

My own method for long putts is quite different than for short putts. Whereas I am looking for firmness and reliability in short-putting, I am looking for a delicate feel in my long-putting. I therefore allow my hands and wrists to come into play far more. With my technique it is obvious when I move from my short-putting method to my long-putting one. As soon as I have a putt of around 20 feet or more I begin to look for accuracy of distance and abandon my cross-handed grip for a conventional one. It depends on the nature of the green at what distance I move from one type of grip and stroke to the other. For middle-distance putts of perhaps 15–25 feet I may see it as a short putt or see it as a long putt. If it is a fairly flat putt with little borrow or distance problems I may stay with my short-putting technique up to 25 feet or so; if there is a very large borrow and a marked upslope or downslope, then I may be somewhat less aggresive about holing the putt and move to my long-putting stroke for something as short as 15 feet. There is a definite kind of in between distance where I may initially have to make a conscious decision over which method to adopt. I am quite sure the majority of tournament professionals do much

106

My long-putting stroke. With the right hand below my left the right shoulder now drops below the left – compare this with my short-putting stroke – and in turn I let the left arm and wrist bend rather more. The hands and wrists come into play for greater feel and sensitive judgement of distance

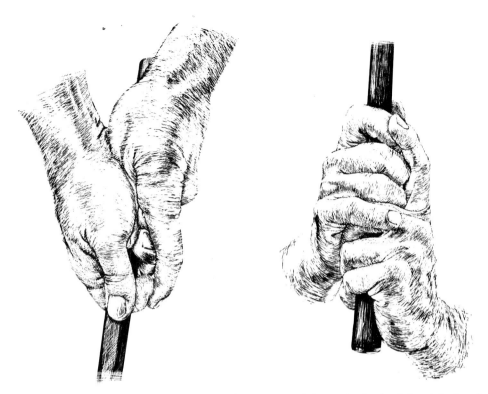

Two views of my grip – the index finger of my left hand down the back of the right hand, which gives feel to the backswing, and the little finger of my right overlapping the second finger of my left

the same thing – at some point they will change from a firm, positive stroke to more of a hand and wrist one. In their case the change is less noticeable but the same decision has been taken.

With long-putting I suggest you use a relatively loose grip, obviously not so loose as to let the putter move in your hands, but free enough to give you a really good feel in the fingertips. Imagine yourself rolling the ball towards the hole with your right hand. You would feel the ball rolling smoothly off your fingertips. With long-putting you have to hold the putter so that you can transmit the feel in your fingertips to the putter head and vice versa. Some people increase this sensitivity by stretching the index finger a little farther down the back of the shaft. It is worth experimenting a little with the grip to try to improve the feel to and from the clubhead.

Most professionals keep much the same address position for long-putting and short-putting, with the eyes still directly over the ball and the stance and body parallel to the line of the putt. Others like to open up a little more by turning the feet slightly towards the hole, in much the same way as one would open up for a short chip or pitch. This may give a clearer

Lee Trevino, with a very orthodox reverse overlap putting grip. Lee, like a number of top players – though not the majority – turns himself slightly towards the target into an open stance in much the same way as most of us do for chipping

view of the line to the hole. Again, it is worth experimenting, particularly if you lack good distance judgement. What you do need to consider is the way you line up a putt and look along it towards the hole. With short-putting the head should very definitely swivel under and up so that the eyes can naturally follow the line. There comes a point in long-putting where for many people this is quite unworkable and they have to lift and turn their heads to see the putt. This varies from one individual to another but may well determine the kind of head position a player adopts for a long putt. It is no good setting your head horizontal if you then find yourself having to lift and turn it to see where you are going. You may need to stand up more and bring the head away from its horizontal position to give yourself a clearer view. Again, it is a matter of trial and error, but it may be a point which you may simply not have thought about before.

The Stroke

We have already seen how much professionals differ over their ideas of putting technique. Usually these differences are far more concerned with short-putting than with long-putting. One of the particular points of difference for short-putting is whether we should consider the putt to be a straight-back-and-through stroke or a naturally curved one. With long-putting we are virtually unanimous in assuming that the clubhead moves back and through on a curved path in just the same way as it does in the full golf swing. A lot of club golfers believe that the putting stroke is straight back and through for any length of putt, with the usual result that the putter head is actually taken slightly outside the line of the putt. With the full golf swing an out-to-in attack is invariably far steeper than an attack from the inside. Just the same applies in putting. I would therefore certainly suggest to any club golfer that he or she checks that the putter head moves back on a low, curved, inside path. The putter head should then return to the ball, travelling in the right direction and with the clubface aimed in the right direction. From here it should naturally return on a slightly curved inside path. It is important that the putter head strikes the ball as close to the ground as possible without actually touching it, that the ball is struck absolutely accurately from the sweet spot of the putter and is set off very accurately in the chosen direction. Providing these principles are met I do not see the stroke itself as being particularly crucial.

Hitting the ball from the sweet spot of the putter is just as vital with long putts as with short putts. You must be quite sure of the spot which gives the solid hit we are looking for. The easiest way of ensuring that you hit the ball with the correct spot is to address the ball from the sweet spot and to look intently at a definite point on the back of the ball through impact, making sure there is no tendency to look up early.

Ben Crenshaw, with a putting stroke that is the envy of many other professionals

Control and Distance

It is sometimes difficult to know what has gone wrong with a long putt left way short or well past the hole. Is it a question of misjudgement or of poor striking? A good depth of contact is vital in setting the ball rolling consistently, getting as near to the ground as possible without ever making contact with it anywhere in the stroke. But what is also important is to be able to control the putt by the length of stroke you use. You cannot be precise over what length of backswing you need for a particular putt. Setting the ball rolling at the correct speed requires a subtle combination of the right length of stroke with rhythm and firmness of strike. Judging the distance you swing the putter should become fairly instinctive. It is much the same as tossing a ball underarm: most of us will quite naturally adjust the swing of the arm without a moment's thought or any careful analysis. But there are two important factors to the length of the putting stroke. First of all, your general principle should be that the backswing and the throughswing are roughly equal, with no tendency to quit on the ball through impact and certainly no tendency to try to jerk the clubhead through. It is a fairly symmetrical arc. The second point is that you can help in producing the right length of backswing by going through a careful routine in setting up to the ball. Having lined up the putt, you should make one or two practice swings in which the main object is to rehearse the length of stroke you want with the ball. Frequently you see players have one or two practice swings which bear no resemblance whatever to the stroke that follows. Bear in mind that it is not the stroke itself and the mechanics which are vital but the judgement of distance.

My pre-shot routine with a long putt includes two practice swings in which I look at the hole and quite definitely imagine the ball running along the right path at the appropriate speed to feel the length of stroke.

It is important to decide exactly what you are trying to achieve. You may, for example, be faced with a virtually straight 30-foot putt on a slow green where you feel aggressive and confident of holing the putt and fairly certain that you are unlikely to charge way past. You may, on the other hand, be faced with a putt which is unpleasantly fast with a lot of borrow, and where, although positive about wanting to hole the putt, your main concern is in lagging it up close to be certain of getting down in two. The situation may change in matchplay or strokeplay according to the state of the game. Try to be specific over the distance you are aiming at rather than just imagining the ball diving into the hole with no concern about

The practice swing for a long putt, looking at the hole and imagining the ball running towards it to give me a feeling for the distance

what might happen if you fail. As a generalization a perfect long putt should finish perhaps 15 inches past the hole for the chance of a single putt but certainty with the second.

Good long-putting, as we have seen, is a question of judgement and feel. It is just as important to practise your long-putting, but instead of working on a precision stroke, work at a very precise control of distance. Reading the greens and selecting a line is a skill all of its own and we will look at that in the next chapter.

8 The Art of Reading Greens

Reading greens well only comes from experience. But many golfers with years of playing the game still have trouble in seeing the breaks and choosing a line.

The Overall Assessment

The first thing we are looking for in reading a putt is simply to assess the overall slope. Is the ground sloping from the right or from the left? You also need to know whether the putt is uphill or downhill or perfectly flat to gauge the speed. Most professional golfers will make an overall assessment of the slopes of a particular green before pinpointing their attention on the putt facing them. It is this initial assessment that I believe

Reading greens starts before you even step on the green. First make an initial assessment of the lie of the land as you approach it. Then if you walk round the green or move aside for your fellow competitor's putt look hard at the overall slope, trying in particular to pinpoint the lowest spot on the green and the general severity of any fall. Things can look quite different from the side and from a distance than from right up to and behind the ball

a lot of amateur golfers fail to make. As you approach the green you should begin to assess the overall lie of the land. Often there is a noticeable fall from one side or the other which is apparent from a distance but which can become difficult to see once you are on the green. Make your initial inspection 20 yards or so from the green. Then, as you move round to leave your clubs to the side or at the back of the green, try again to get an overall picture of the contours. It is worth trying to assess which is the highest point of the green and which the lowest point, and then, if you have to mark your ball and wait for your partners to putt, make some general observations from the lowest point to judge the degree of slope. As a rule professional golfers go through this kind of process in a practice round to see the green in its entirety. This is particularly important on greens where there may be a very large borrow which is not always apparent when reading the putt from close range.

Three-Point Reading

This overall assessment of the green also tells me where I want to make my first inspection of a particular putt. I look at the putt from three angles, and my first viewpoint is from the side below the putt. At this point I make my judgement as to whether the putt is uphill or downhill. Do not be fooled into thinking you can accurately assess an upslope or downslope from behind the ball: quite frequently the eyes will deceive you from this foreshortened angle. If time permits, look at the ball from the side, this will give you your clues as to the speed of the putt as well as help you gauge more accurately its overall distance.

On both a short putt and a long putt I then move behind the hole to take a view from this angle. **The view from behind the hole can be extremely important. Remember that the ball will always break most when it is slowing down, i.e. when it is near the hole, and it is this area which usually has most influence on the ball.** The ball travels relatively quickly over the first two thirds of a putt and will often take far less break than you expect. As it approaches the hole and slows down, any little irregularity comes into play. The slower the ball is travelling the more crucial the contours. From this angle you should try to see which side of the hole is higher and picture where the ball should drop in. Some players also look at the way in which the hole has been cut. If it has been cut perfectly vertically it is worth looking to see whether there is more earth showing above one side of the inner cup than the other. If there is more on one side than the other, then this side is higher. Depending on the way

I read my putts from three angles: from the side I can see the upslope or downslope; from behind the hole I can see the irregularities nearest the hole which will affect the ball when it is slowing down; and from this third view I can judge the overall line and choose my aiming spot

in which the hole has been cut, this view can give you information about what is going to happen in the crucial zone near the hole.

The third angle of looking at the putt is from directly behind the ball. Most golfers limit their reading of greens to a view taken from this direction. If you simply look at the putt from here without walking the length of the putt you will find that the distance is foreshortened, and, as a consequence you may fail to judge it properly and to make an accurate assessment of whether the putt is uphill or downhill. But from here you should be looking for the overall slope of the putt and picking out the line on which you want to start the ball. You will get a fair idea of the slopes involved standing 6 feet or so behind the ball; then by squatting down at this sort of distance you will be able to make a more accurate assessment. It is often a mistake to get too close to the ball when reading the putt; the closer you get to it the more you are looking *down* at the ground rather than looking *along* the ground. Sometimes you may find it helpful to move even farther away and to get as low as possible for a really good view at a fairly horizontal angle.

116

Sometimes it is easier to see the line of a putt from further away for a better overall impression and a more horizontal view of the ground

Obviously for a club player there are dangers in becoming too slow by taking this three-point view. I do, however, think that many club players do not make the most of the opportunity to look for more information and could easily study the putt from different angles while other players in the group prepare for their putts.

Plumb-bobbing

You will often see professional golfers reading greens by hanging the putter vertically in front of them, the toe of the putter either directly towards or away from them. If the player does this from a squatting position behind the ball he is usually simply giving himself a vertical line as an extra point of reference for judging the slopes of the horizon. This

Giving myself a vertical reference for judging the slope of the hole

118

can be a useful aid with hilly courses where the greens and overall contours of the ground can be deceptive and you lose all idea of the true horizontal.

The player who stands directly behind the ball and then hangs the putter in front of him is usually using a different technique which is generally known as 'plumb-bobbing'. To use this technique you need to know which is your master eye. Hold your index finger out at arm's length in front of you. Look at it with both eyes. Now close your left eye and see whether your finger seems to have moved relative to its background. Look again with both eyes and then close your right eye. When looking with your master eye and the other one closed there will be less movement.

Now to the plumb-bobbing exercise. Stand 4 feet or so directly behind the ball; lining up accurately is important. You should position the feet apart, with the ball not quite opposite the middle of the stance but opposite

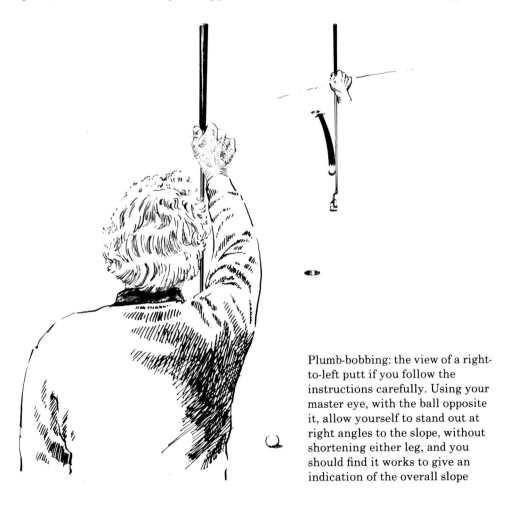

Plumb-bobbing: the view of a right-to-left putt if you follow the instructions carefully. Using your master eye, with the ball opposite it, allow yourself to stand out at right angles to the slope, without shortening either leg, and you should find it works to give an indication of the overall slope

your master eye. What is also important is that you stand at right angles to any slope you feel beneath your feet and do *not* shorten either leg to bring yourself into an upright position. Make an assumption as to whether the putt will break in from the right or the left. Let us assume it will move in from the right. With your non-master eye closed, hang the putter vertically in front of you with the thumb and index finger of either hand. Viewing the putter and ball with your master eye, bring the putter into a position so that it appears to touch the right side of the ball a few inches up from the head of the club. Now look at the hole and compare its visual position with the top of the putter shaft. If the hole seems displaced to the left and is not touching the shaft, this indicates that indeed the putt will break from right to left. The closer the hole seems to the putter shaft the more likely it is to be a straight putt. If both ball and hole seem to line up well with the putter shaft it may be a fairly straight putt, but you can check this by taking a reading with the putter shaft hanging to the left of the ball and seeing whether the hole seems to move away from the right of the shaft. What you are in effect measuring is the angle of the slope on which you are standing. It does not necessarily reveal what happens near the hole, but it is a method used by many good putters, mainly as a way of checking greens with severe and somewhat confusing slopes.

Allowing for the Break – Long Putts

Having looked at the putt from one, two or three angles, you should have an accurate idea of the slopes involved. The amount you allow for a sideslope will depend on the speed of the putt. When a putt is fast the break will be much more severe than when the green is slow. Greens like those at Augusta and at other major championships tend to be set up to be far quicker than for normal play, making them even more difficult and critical to read. The way in which you aim to allow for the borrow is important, but professionals by no means all do it the same way.

First of all let us look at a 30-foot putt of medium pace when you know there is a very slight slope from the right. In this case the borrow is going to be so small that I would simply choose a spot to the side of the hole and aim directly at that. **It is important that the spot you choose is absolutely specific. I sometimes hear inexperienced caddies or amateur golfers saying they will aim 'about 3 inches right'. The word 'about' should not enter your vocabulary! It is either 3 inches right or it is not 3 inches right.** You should choose a definite spot, perhaps some little irregularity on the green, and then visualize that as

Choosing an aiming spot needs to be precise. On a short putt or on a longish one with very little borrow, I usually aim by reference to a spot directly to the side of the hole. This can be to some little irregularity on the green if there is one. If not I usually imagine a number of golf balls beside the hole and aim my ball for one of those. I then see it as a straight putt to the chosen spot and virtually ignore the hole

strongly as you would visualize the hole on a perfectly straight putt. I like to have a picture in my mind to aim at and will often aim in relation to the width of a hole or the width of a ball. In this situation I might, for example, visualize three golf balls sitting to the right of the hole and aim my putt directly in the centre of the third ball. I might, on the other hand, visualize a golf hole to the right of the real one and aim for the right of that imaginary hole. I do not think in terms of inches or centimetres, but always in terms of hole- or ball-width, which is very precise visually. Whichever way you do it, the spot you aim at must be definite and your putting stroke must be directed at that. Forget the hole and concentrate on the spot.

With a long putt like this it is helpful, if you are having the flag attended, for your caddie or playing partner to stand on the higher side of the hole. This will give you some point of reference for bringing the ball in past his feet. When there is a relatively small break you may find you can aim directly at one of his feet, though it would, of course, be a breach of the rules to position him, or for him to position himself, with the idea of giving you a specific aiming point. There is no harm in matchplay in asking your opponent to attend the flag on whichever side of the hole you wish.

You can allow for a break by choosing an intermediate spot in several ways. Having chosen the aiming spot forget about the overall curve and visualize the ball travelling *straight* to your chosen spot

a) Here I am aiming to pass the ball directly over a certain spot. That means aiming slightly to the side of it to allow for a little break before it gets there

b) This time I am aiming to an intermediate spot but know that the ball will take up a little break and won't actually pass right over it

c) In this case I am just trying to start the ball off on line by choosing a spot on the beginning of the curve

Now let us look at another putt of 30 feet, but this time with a substantial break in from the right on a very fast green. With this I do not believe the correct way would be to choose a spot, say, 4 feet to the right of the hole and level with it. This to me would be relatively meaningless. I would choose an intermediate spot, perhaps threequarters of the way along the putt, and visualize the ball running straight to that spot and then curving in a pronounced way down towards the hole.

As I have already explained, the ball takes up most of its break when it slows down, in other words in the last third or quarter. It is therefore true to say that the ball will run almost straight for the first threequarters of the distance before taking up the break – but it will not run absolutely straight. The way you choose the intermediate spot needs careful consideration for real accuracy. Are you choosing a spot knowing that in reality the ball will have broken down the slope slightly before it reaches it, so that it passes it on the low side? Or do you actually mean the ball to pass over the spot and break in from there? If the latter, then in reality you will be aiming above it to allow for a little break in the first three-quarters. Make sure you differentiate between the two. If a caddie gives you a line to a specific point en route, does he mean you to aim at it or come in over it? The difference on a normal green may be an inch or so (still enough to miss), but on slick tournament greens the two are not the same at all. If you mean to bring the ball in over a spot, then your stroke needs to aim the ball 1, 2, 3 or however many inches above that spot.

A slightly different way of seeing this putt would be to visualize the whole curve of the putt as though traced on the green in front of you and then to start the ball off along that curve without any real choice of an intermediate spot. In this case aiming the putt would be much more a matter of choosing a spot on the beginning of that curve just 18 inches or so in front of you and trying to start the ball accurately out over that.

What seems to happen with players who do not read long swinging putts correctly is that they select a line with far too little borrow and then do not actually start the ball out in the chosen direction, frequently borrowing much more but still not enough. It seems that this is through failing to visualize the whole course the ball will take, particularly in the area near the hole. With a severe slope the ball may stop moving forward and may start running sharply downhill, almost at right angles as you look at it. It is important to plan any sharply swinging putt, long or short, with the idea of the ball dropping in from directly above the hole. It is definitely wrong to visualize the ball dropping in the front entrance. You will almost certainly be underborrowing and will never keep the ball high enough.

Allowing for the Break – Short Putts

Ideally with a short putt of perhaps 8 feet or less I like to be able to choose an aiming spot at or just outside the edge of the hole. I visualize this spot quite distinctly, either finding some little mark on the green or imagining one or more balls to the side and aiming in relation to those. With a slightly breaking putt the speed is not too critical, providing the ball has enough speed to hold its line. Remember that the last 6 inches of roll are the danger zone where all the little irregularities and the slope take real effect. I want to hold my line but leave no more than a 15-inch return putt if I should miss. Direction is more vital than speed.

With a short sidehill putt on a very fast green the choice of line has to be linked to speed. The more softly you stroke the ball, the more break it takes but the safer if you should miss. The firmer you can be the less break you need allow for. Practise both types of approach. The aggressive one has its place even for the most cautious of players, particularly in matchplay with a putt for a half. But do be certain that a caddy or partner reading the green with you knows how softly or firmly you are thinking of playing it. Strength and line must go together.

As the sideslope increases and the green gets faster the consideration of speed and direction becomes critical. I am sure by now you appreciate that a ball struck firmly and travelling fast holds its line; one travelling slowly takes up the break. With a breaking putt on a fast green the ball has to be stroked gently to avoid overshooting, and because of this slow speed the ball breaks substantially. In extreme cases you may need to allow for it to break by the hole almost at right angles to the ball–hole line. Speed becomes absolutely crucial to ensure that the break is right at the hole, rather than in front of or past it. I invariably continue to choose an aiming point to the side but level with the hole, finding that this encourages precise distance judgement. Some players prefer to select some intermediate spot, well up the slope, setting the ball off with just the right speed for it to die down into the highest edge of the hole.

As I have explained before, the more boldly you strike the ball the better it holds its line. If you attack the hole aggressively, the break can be treated as relatively small, but the results will be disastrous if you should miss. If you trickle the ball slowly with safety in mind, the break is substantial. It is important to realize that the situation can dictate the approach. If you are not particularly concerned about the one back if you should miss, the putt can be seen as relatively straight and attacked firmly. This could well be the approach to take with a putt to tie for a championship. If it were to miss, the difference between second and third place might seem inconsequential. This would certainly be the approach for a putt to save a half in a match. What is important is that you practise both types of approach – bold and safe. It is easy to take an aggressive line on the practice green, with little or no concern for the one back, and then to tackle putts quite differently in a competitive situation.

Starting the Ball on Line

In selecting a line for a long putt, or indeed a short putt, there will always be an element of choice as to which spot to aim for. This will either be to the side of the hole, or perhaps two thirds of the way along the putt, or possibly only 18 inches ahead of you if starting the ball off along a curve. To my mind you should then think in terms of a straight line to that spot and see your putting stroke in relation to that line. I mention this because a lot of players look at a breaking putt only in terms of a curve and then produce a rather haphazard putting stroke which possibly follows the kind of curve of the putt with no real idea of sending the ball off in a straight line. This can be particularly disastrous with short putts. Instead of a stroke which follows the line to the aiming spot, the player loses the stroke altogether on a short putt with a borrow. **Having chosen your aiming point, treat each putt as a straight putt to that spot and produce your normal stroke with that point (and not the hole) in mind.**

Many players with a breaking short putt find either the right-to-left putt or the left-to-right putt far more difficult than the other. I feel more comfortable with the right-to-left one. Another reason for feeling awkward over the stroke with a short putt is that your feet may well be an inch or so below or above the ball. If you are standing below the ball it is likely to push your feet farther from the ball and produce a more curved path to

Sideslope putts can throw the stroke out of line. On a right-to-left slope with your feet a little below the ball there may be a tendency to stand a little further from it, just as in the long game. Some players allow for this by playing the ball a little more towards the toe of the putter to keep it up the slope

126

the stroke; above the ball, you may be inclined to move closer to it with your eyes outside the line. The changes are minute but need understanding. The path may change unsuitably on a breaking putt without particular care and attention to your aiming line. There are some professionals who make a slight compensation for the possible changes by no longer using the exact sweet spot of the putter. Fuzzy Zoeller is one who springs to mind, seeming to hit right-to-left putts from the toe of the putter, presumably with the idea of holding the ball up to the right, and conversely hitting the ball a little out of the heel with a left-to-right putt. It is not a method I use but it may be of help.

Conversely, on a left-to-right putt with the feet a little above the ball, there are some players who advocate keeping the ball a little more towards the heel of the putter to keep it up to the left

Judging Grain

Another point which should come into your reading of greens is the grain of the grass, in other words the direction in which it grows. In Germany and the rest of northern Europe where I learned my golf, grain is not really a factor which you need to take into account, other than possibly being aware of the effects of the direction of cutting. But in many golfing countries the grain needs careful consideration; on some courses good reading and understanding of the grain can be just as or more important than reading the slopes.

For those golfers who have no real concept of grain on greens it is worth looking first at the effect which a mower has on the appearance of grass. The neat mower lines produced by an ordinary cylinder mower are simply the result of the grass being pushed in one direction with the first cut and in the opposite direction with the second. A mower cut travelling away from you leaves the grass looking relatively pale and shiny, and one towards you leaves the grass looking much deeper in colour but dull in texture.

On courses in North America, the Far East, Africa and southern Europe the various kinds of grass differ in the way they grow and do not necessarily stand upright. Sometimes grass will tend to grow towards the setting sun, towards the sea or other areas of water, in the direction of the prevailing wind, away from certain mountains or simply in the direction in which most people walk across the green. Very often the whole green will appear shiny in one direction and dull in the other direction. If you are putting with the grain, in other words, when it looks shiny, the ball will tend to run much more quickly. If putting uphill, the grain may almost nullify the effect of the slope; if putting downhill and with the grain, the putt becomes lightning fast. If putting against the grain with the grass looking dark and dull, the putt will be much slower. A downslope may have little effect and an uphill putt becomes exaggeratedly slow. Where the grain runs across the line of the putt treat it in just the same way as a sideslope, allowing for the ball to curve in with the grain. Again, where there is a combination of slope and grain you need to take extra care. A right-to-left slope with the grain running left to right may need to be treated as a straight putt. Where slope and grain go in the same direction the effect is severe.

Sometimes the effect of the grain can be seen quite clearly because of the apparent colour of the grass. But in some instances it is far less apparent and the direction in which the grass grows can only be determined by careful examination. Sometimes it is worth looking at the area

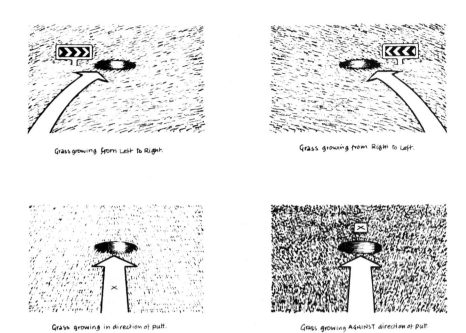

Grass growing from Left to Right.

Grass growing from Right to Left.

Grass growing in direction of putt.

Grass growing AGAINST direction of putt.

On some greens allowing for grain can be just as important as allowing for the slope, whether aiming off to the side to allow for it or judging the speed of a putt from the shininess or dullness of the grass growing away from or towards you

Looking at the edge of the hole can reveal the direction of the grain. The blades of grass may seem to overhang the hole slightly on one side, with a bare part where the grass seems to grow away from it

immediately around the hole, the direction of growth showing at the hole itself with the blades of grass clearly appearing to be thick and overhanging the hole on one side and yet growing away from it and leaving a pronounced bare spot on the other. Another way of examining the grain can be to look at the grass just off the edge of the green where there may be an area cut at a very slightly higher level; the direction of the growth of the grass may then be seen quite clearly.

Professional golfers usually take great pains in a practice round to examine the nature of the grain. In a practice round I will often run my putter head across the green to see if the grass seems to lie in a particular direction; it may feel smooth in one direction and rough in the other. Under the rules you can of course only do this in practice and not in play. Another way of testing the grain is to take a fairly flat putt, hitting the ball in one direction and then hitting it in the opposite direction to see if it clearly runs at different speeds. Quite often the professional or experienced caddies at a course can give a very clear indication of the way in which the grass grows and you have to trust this after confirming it for yourself in practice rounds. If you find yourself on a green which clearly has some form of grain but you cannot work out the prevailing direction, first look to see whether the grass grows away from mountains or towards the sea. If that does not provide the answer look for some directional clue, perhaps it grows towards the setting sun in the west or the southwest, or perhaps it simply grows with the downslope.

Once you have judged the grain, have the confidence to allow for it. It may either exaggerate or minimize the effect of a slope and in extreme cases you may even find that your putt travels slightly uphill with the grain rather than downhill with the slope!

Using Your Practice Rounds

The tournament golfer needs to learn a lot about the greens on a particular course in either one or two practice rounds. Most club golfers get to know the greens on their home course through years of experience and generally figure out the slopes through trial and error. But the tournament professional has to learn quickly. In practice rounds I make accurate notes not only of the yardage to the green but also of any deceptive slopes or the direction of grain.

What other points do I look for? I look carefully at the way in which a chip or long putt rolls as it passes the hole to get an indication of what will happen on the way back. I look very carefully at the way in which my partner's putt breaks to see if I can learn from it. In a practice round I certainly won't necessarily putt to the hole. The hole is usually cut at the front or middle of the green for a practice round and not where it is likely to be in the tournament itself. In practice I may well ignore the flag in hitting into the green, and I usually pick out various corners of the green to try putts to likely pin positions. In this way I cover as much of the green as possible to get a really good idea of all the slopes. I also look at any

The experienced golfer begins to recognize clues around the green to indicate differences of speed and texture

a) A plateau green may drain more quickly through the day than the rest and be faster

b) A green in a bowl may hold and gather water. Long shots to it may stop more easily and the green remain slower, with thicker grass

c) Overhanging trees may leave one part of the green in shadow throughout the day, never drying out and remaining moist and slow

d) A large tree or trees near a green may throw up roots and drain it of moisture and goodness. Watch for an irregular area with less grass

overhanging trees or drainage problems. Sometimes this can give a clue to a green whose speed is different from the others. Overhanging trees may leave the green in shadow all day with the grass drying out slowly and the green staying slower. Sometimes trees can have a different effect, with the roots taking the goodness from the grass and the growth being uneven and the green unpredictable. A green which forms a raised plateau may drain too well and become faster than the others; a green in a bowl may gather water and stay slow. It is worth finding out whether any greens have been relaid within the last couple of years. This may result in a slower green than the others. For tournament players these extra obser-

vations can produce added information to explain inconsistencies from one green to another. But if some extra thought like this saves a stroke or two over seventy-two holes it can make all the difference between winning a major championship and the oblivion of being runner-up.

Check Your Reading

Good reading of the greens, as we have seen, is just as important as a good stroke and in long-putting perhaps more so. The difficulty is that, when a putt is missed, the player is often uncertain whether he has read the putt wrongly or struck the ball poorly. In a practice round check your reading, if necessary by repeating a failed putt and adjusting the line. But I would also recommend that you get a friend or your caddie to check whether you really do start the ball off on the line you have chosen. Many players do not start the ball accurately on their chosen line for a long putt and do not know the reason for failure. Nominate your chosen line, position your caddie beyond the hole and let him check your starting point. In this way you can begin to determine whether it is the reading or the stroke which is at fault.

Opposite: Jack Nicklaus and Jack Jr. Two pairs of eyes can be better than one, even for the greatest! It is useful, too, to have someone checking whether you really do start the putt on the chosen line. This indicates whether your reading or striking needs attention

9 Precision Practice

Good putting requires just as much practice as the rest of the golf game. Bearing in mind that putting can be 30–40 per cent of the whole game, it perhaps warrants almost more practice than anything else. This chapter contains several ideas for routines to help you and tips on what to do when things go wrong.

The Short-Putt Stroke

A good way of grooving the putting stroke, if you think of it as a straight line rather than a curve, is to lay out a couple of club shafts and to swing the putter back and through between them. For some it may be more satisfactory to use one single club outside the putter, as this prevents a bad outward movement but allows a slight inward curve. You can do this either on a carpet or with a short, straight putt on the green.

I like to start my practice putting sessions with a few minutes' work on a straight putt of about 3 feet. This gives me confidence and helps me to build up the initial stroke. From this length there is no need for any head or eye movement to see the ball drop, and this helps promote the feeling of staying really still.

To practise the reading of your short putts and make something slightly competitive, a good routine is to position six balls around the hole in a circle at the same distance and to try to hole these in turn. Some are going to be right to left, others left to right, and there should be a certain degree of motivation in trying to hole each one, rehearsing your ambitions on the course. Start with a circle of 3-foot putts – roughly putter length – and then gradually move out to a circle of 6–8 feet. But don't ignore the 3–4 foot ones. This is the critical holing-out length you may well keep leaving yourself after a slightly wayward long putt or a good chip.

Grooving the putting stroke along another club shaft

Increasing Your Accuracy

If you get used to practising to a small target it can make the hole seem relatively large and a putt fairly simple! You can easily do this by putting to one tee, by setting two tees $2\frac{1}{2}$ inches apart and trying to putt between them, or by putting on your carpet to an inverted tee or a matchbox. In a similar way, you can increase the demands of a putt by positioning a couple of tees to block off part of the hole.

Another point to check is whether you hit the ball truly with the sweet spot of your putter. You can monitor this a few times in practice by putting a blob of paint or chalk on the back of the ball and seeing where it leaves a mark on your putter face. To help in hitting the ball from the sweet spot, try marking the face of the putter with a small piece of sticky paper – the size of a very small coin – and watch carefully to see if you hit the ball with it. You will probably be able to *feel* the difference with the paper in position.

Left-Hand Control

One of the key principles which most good putters have in common is that the left wrist and arm stay constant through impact. Most tournament professionals, if not ambidextrous, at least have good strength and control with their left hand and arm in long shots. Part of your putting practice routine should be to build up an accurate stroke with the left hand alone, learning to roll in putts of 3–4 feet. This should stop you developing an overdominant right hand, particularly if you practise with the left hand for a few putts and then add the right one while the left still feels active.

Another exercise is to practise a push stroke, with no backswing at all. This is an illegal stroke and only a practice technique. The push stroke means that you have to learn acceleration and an accurate throughstroke. This exercise is particularly helpful for the player who tends to swing the putter too far back and then to slow down.

Left-handed practice to encourage a solid left wrist through impact

136

Varying the Length

I like practice routines which have a slightly competitive element. These can be particularly useful for players who find it difficult to putt under pressure. Another exercise of this kind is to position six balls in a line, the first approximately 2 feet away from the hole and the rest at 1-foot intervals. Start with the first, move on to the second, then on to the third and so on. If you miss one, then take all the balls out of the hole and start again. It may be quite difficult to sink the fifth or sixth putt, but once you do hole all six, move on to slightly longer putts – 4 feet and upwards – with the same idea in mind. Again, this seems to help players to keep the head still. I suppose that turning one's thoughts to the next ball in the line tends to stop movement up and forwards through impact.

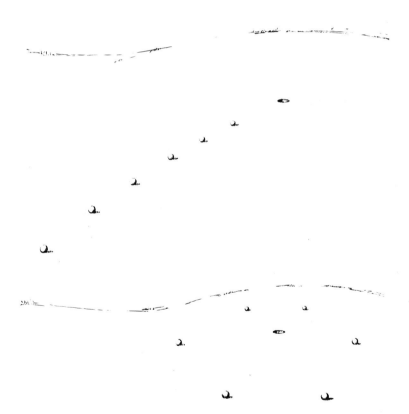

Two putting exercises to add a little pressure. With the line of balls from about 2 to 10 feet start with the closest, back to the second, then to the third and so on. If you miss one, start again. A circle of balls equidistant from the hole requires good reading of the slopes. As you go round the circle the line changes, giving a variety of putts

137

Judging Distance

When we come on to long putts, judging distance becomes crucial. After starting my pre-round practice session with short putts to groove the stroke, I always follow up with some long putts, not from one spot to the same hole, but varying the length of each to get a feel for the speed of the greens. Amateur golfers often ignore this part of practice, possibly thinking that the practice green may be different from those on the course and that little is to be gained by it. But you can develop feel for distance on virtually any reasonably good green, and on days when you cannot get on the course you can even benefit from practice on an expanse of carpet.

A good routine is to take three balls, hit the first, and then try to repeat this distance for the second and third ball without actually looking up after the first putt. If your striking of the ball is accurate with good depth contact and from the middle of the putter, all three balls should finish at much the same length. If the length differs by more than 18 inches, it may give you some clue that the depth of strike is poor. The length of the putt should be governed by the length of the stroke, and if this remains constant the putts should be accurate for length. Always play and practise with the same brand of ball. The different covers and cores of golf balls can give slight variations in the feel of clubhead to ball, with possible discrepancies in the speed of roll.

You can soon think up your own ways of developing distance control. An idea which you can try out on a carpet is to place on the floor two pieces of thread perhaps 1 foot apart and to practise trying to stop the balls between the two. You can try much the same on the green, laying out a couple of pieces of string or setting tees in the ground to give yourself a distance 'box' to aim for.

To practise good distance judgement set another club down about 2 feet behind the hole, trying to stop each putt that does miss between the hole and club

Another idea is to practise putting to a hole with another golf club 2 feet behind the hole, with the aim of your putts finishing somewhere between the hole (if they miss) and the other club. It is worth thinking of routines and exercises which appeal to you.

Long-Putt Practice

As well as practising distance control, it is vital that you check and practise your reading of the greens. Take time on the practice green to go through the routine of reading greens rather than just making a guess at the line and then adjusting your second or third putt accordingly. Try to make the correct judgement the first time; that, after all, is what you have to do on the course.

You can simply practise long-putting by going round the putting green and trying to cover the nine or eighteen holes in as few shots as possible, holing out *everything*. But if you have the putting green to yourself you can work on an infinite variety of long putts, reading each carefully and going from a putt of one length to one of another so that you get practice on both line and length. You need to check your reading accurately, again being very specific over your choice of an aiming spot, nominating exactly where you are lining up, and having someone else checking the line on which the ball starts. Try to get to the point where you nominate the correct line and start the ball along it. This should avoid the trial and error of a missed putt in which you don't know whether the stroke or the reading is at fault.

Practising Your Routine

As I have stressed throughout the book, it is essential to adopt a routine and to keep to it in all situations. This encompasses the precise way in which you read the green, choose your line, take your practice swings and approach the whole putt. This routine needs patient practice, gradually making your method into a definite habit and reinforcing the muscle memory. By carefully repeating the preparation for each putt the muscles are brought into action in an identical manner time and again, with the maximum chance of repeating the stroke itself precisely.

In normal practice conditions and during the pre-round warm-up I repeat the stroke precisely but do not always go through the whole routine of lining up the putt from three angles, having my set number of practice swings and so on. But there are times when it is necessary to take each putt slowly and carefully through a practice session to build the routine. It is worth spending time over certain putts, imagining each is in an important tournament, and going through the whole meticulous process of lining them up and carrying out your pre-shot routine in just the same way as you would on the course. Don't putt at one speed on the practice green and then change this on the course. See it as a definite part of your practice until you could almost set a stopwatch to time your putting routine from start to finish.

What To Do When Things Go Wrong

In many ways the time to practise putting is when things are going well and you can accurately groove a good stroke. Amateur golfers seem to ignore practice unless they have problems. The more you can practise your stroke when the going is good, the better. But when problems arise you need to have some definite ideas to work on to try to solve the problems. As we saw early on in the book, much of the problem with putting is that the reasons for a missed putt can be many and varied. Is the putt which consistently misses to the left the result of a closed clubface, a putt hit from out of the heel, a tendency to aim left or simply an off-line stroke? If you have a consistent fault with short-putting then your path to improvement needs to be systematic. Don't try adjusting several variables at the same time. Work at one at a time and you will gradually discover the fault. Always check first the clubface to see whether you really are forming a right angle to your target. Then check the sweet spot of the putter, having made sure you know exactly where it is; then ensure that you are setting up and hitting the ball from the correct spot. If you begin to suspect that you are starting to hit the ball out of the toe or the heel, then try the reverse action to see if this eliminates the bad effect. In other words, go through the principles set out earlier in the book and take each in turn in a precise and analytical way until you find the fault.

Of more concern are the times when you seem to produce an inconsistent fault, putts which miss sometimes to the left and sometimes to the right. Here the problem is more likely one of producing a poor roll to the ball which fails to keep it travelling smoothly. Check that the grip really is returning the clubface squarely and look at what happens to the stroke beyond impact. Is the putter correctly going through towards the hole – if it is the ball should roll smoothly – or is it tending to cut across and pull in towards your feet? A good way of checking this roll is to use a ball with a stripe marked around it, lining up the stripe with the hole, and trying

140

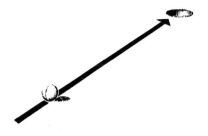

Using a ball painted with a stripe, with the stripe aimed at the hole, can give an indication as to whether the ball is set rolling truly or whether it wobbles from unwanted sidespin

A practice technique to encourage an aggressive attack – trying to hit the tee peg in the back of the hole

to see it rolling over and over quite smoothly. If you think that inconsistencies in the green might be responsible for any problems, try the same experiment on a carpet to develop the feeling of the ball rolling accurately. The form of your stroke can make a surprising difference to the way in which the ball rolls, and the less wobble you see to the stripe mark the better.

With general problems of inconsistency I would also look at the depth of contact. Are you striking the ball solidly at its back, or is there a tendency to hit the ball too high up or, almost more disastrous, to scuff the ground? This can produce a bad roll, but it can also cause poor and inconsistent judgement of distance. Check that the weight of the putter is supported by your arms and hands, and *not* resting on the ground, before the stroke starts, but with the grip pressure light to encourage smoothness.

Where there is general inconsistency with short putts and no definite pattern at all, I would also suggest checking the speed and distance of the putt. A putt which is dying into the hole is going to take up maximum break just around the hole. Check whether a putt that misses really is going to finish about 15 inches past; this should give the maximum chance of holding the line without having to borrow excessively, but should also leave you in a position from which the return putt is a formality. Be certain that you really are aggressive enough with the short putts. A practice technique to encourage an aggressive attack is to stick a tee peg in the back of the cup and to try to get the feeling of the ball striking the tee rather than just dribbling in the front of the hole.

Head Position

If you are finding difficulties with your short-putting, check your head position to ensure that your eyes are directly over the ball and the eye line parallel to the putt, or at least in the position which you know produces your best results. As a reminder, if the eyes tend to be inside the line there can be a tendency to push the ball, and if outside, then a tendency to pull it.

At the first sign of putting problems check your eye position relative to the ball – the standard position being directly above or fractionally inside it

Last of all in fault finding with putting, remember the advice of so many good putters that keeping the head still is perhaps the most important key to putting and that looking up too soon is the most common cause of a missed putt. Practise repeatedly trying to hole short and medium-length putts, while keeping your head perfectly still and listening for the ball to drop in, rather than following it with your eyes or moving your head. An excellent way of encouraging the head to stay still, and also to produce the very best stroke possible, is to adopt a stroke in which the putter swings back, through and back to address before looking up. It focuses the mind on the ball and the spot it has left for a moment after impact, and will also make you realize if the throughswing is being pulled off line. If you can achieve this on the practice green it should at least mean that you keep your head still for a second or so beyond impact when under pressure in a competitive situation.

10 Psychology and Strategy

Good putting depends to a large extent on developing a sound stroke, practising this religiously to withstand pressure and then learning the art of reading greens. But it does not stop there. To be a really good putter you have to have the right mental approach to cope with pressure and disappointments and to understand the way in which your mind can help or hinder your game. People say that putting is all in the mind, but that is undoubtedly an exaggeration. Your method has to be good, but in order to use it to its full potential there is no doubt that you have to think correctly and understand your mental weaknesses.

Imagination

Your eyes play a very important part in putting, perhaps almost more so than in the rest of the game. You have to have a good eye for reading greens, for judging distance and for setting the putter squarely to your target. You also need to be able to use your imagination as you look at any putt to 'see' certain clues to lining up and producing a good stroke. I explained earlier, for example, how I line up a putt by aiming to the right or left of the hole and visualizing one, two or three golf balls sitting to the side of the hole, aiming my ball to the outermost of the imaginary balls. The picture in my mind is extremely clear, almost as though the balls were actually sitting there. I am sure that a vivid imagination plays a part in the game of any good putter. Obviously we cannot get inside other people's minds to know exactly what happens, but I would guess that all professional golfers 'see' a clearly marked curve on the green tracing the path of a putt, or 'see' a bold, clear line on which to start the ball. I expect that imagination varies from one person to another, and possibly some readers find it hard to visualize aiming spots or putting paths. But these are essential ingredients of good putting and with practice the images can become more vivid.

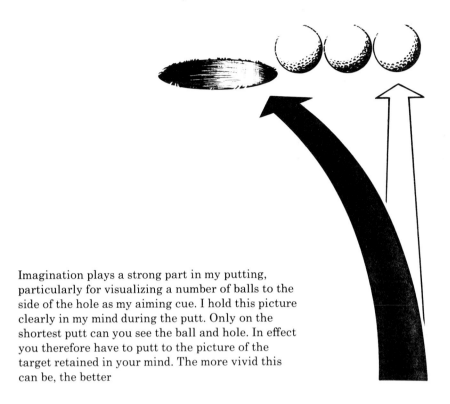

Imagination plays a strong part in my putting, particularly for visualizing a number of balls to the side of the hole as my aiming cue. I hold this picture clearly in my mind during the putt. Only on the shortest putt can you see the ball and hole. In effect you therefore have to putt to the picture of the target retained in your mind. The more vivid this can be, the better

Imagination is also important to me when I am lining up a putt and making my practice swings to rehearse my stroke and gauge distance. With the long putt my concentration is probably largely focused on rehearsing the right length of stroke to send the ball the correct distance. I visualize the ball running at the correct speed along the chosen path to the hole, and this gives my body the necessary clues to producing the right length of swing. With a short putt in the moments before I make the critical stroke I have to imagine the ball following the proper path and falling neatly into the hole. Now the line is almost more crucial than the distance. For the experienced player these pictures in the mind serve as a kind of instruction. If I imagine the ball running a certain length on a long putt, I produce the right length of stroke fairly instinctively. I do not have to think of swinging the putter back so many inches or through so many inches, but the very thought of the ball running a set distance tells my body what to do. It becomes just like throwing a ball. **If you throw a ball underarm to a target you simply look at the target, your brain in a split second gauges the length of throw and weight of object, and your arms and hands produce a surprisingly accurate result. Just**

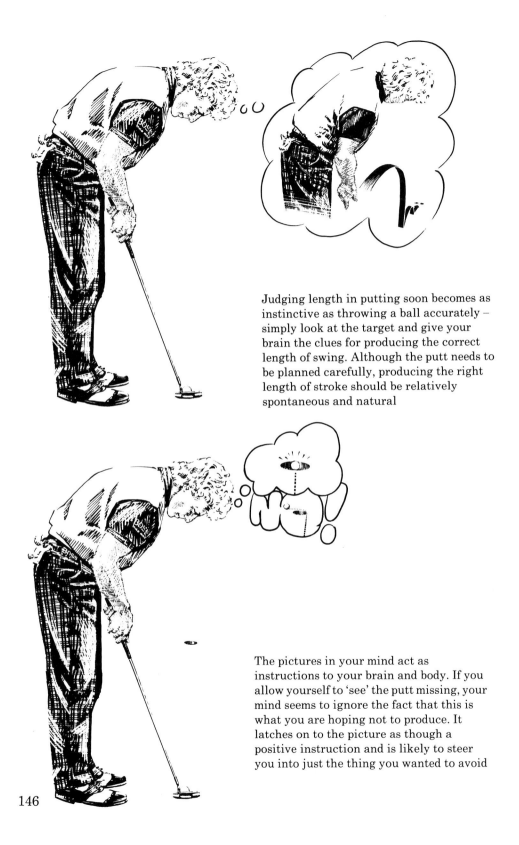

Judging length in putting soon becomes as instinctive as throwing a ball accurately – simply look at the target and give your brain the clues for producing the correct length of swing. Although the putt needs to be planned carefully, producing the right length of stroke should be relatively spontaneous and natural

The pictures in your mind act as instructions to your brain and body. If you allow yourself to 'see' the putt missing, your mind seems to ignore the fact that this is what you are hoping not to produce. It latches on to the picture as though a positive instruction and is likely to steer you into just the thing you wanted to avoid

the same thing happens in putting. It works in exactly the same way for direction, the mental pictures giving your brain the instructions to perform the right stroke. The danger comes when you allow yourself to have negative thoughts and produce pictures of what you don't want.

Positive Thinking

Whenever you play any shot in golf, from a short putt up to a full drive, the pictures which you produce in your mind are crucial in making your body respond in the right way. A good golfer playing, for example, a 60-yard pitch will look at the target and instinctively produce the right length of swing. If I want to fade the ball round some trees I need do very little other than visualize the ball bending left to right, and this will help to key me in to the right movements. The problems arise when you cannot get the right picture in your mind and your thoughts become negative. If you stand on a tee and imagine your ball hooking out of bounds to the left, the odds are that that is what you will do. If you imagine yourself topping a ball into a lake, you have little chance of a good shot. **The pictures in your mind must be positive, not negative. It is as though your brain cannot distinguish between pictures of what you do want to do and of what you don't want to do, and if you picture the thing you are trying to avoid your brain does its level best to make it happen!**

The same thing happens on the green with just as devastating results. If you set up to a putt of 4 feet and keep imagining that you are going to miss it on the left, then almost certainly you will. If all you can 'see' is the ball pushed away past the right lip, then again, you don't have much chance of success. If, on the other hand, you can produce the right picture of the ball running on the correct path and diving into the hole, then it won't make you infallible – nothing will – but it will help bring out the best in your stroke.

The main difficulty for people who putt badly is that they keep getting the wrong picture and may, for example, stand over every short putt quite unable to 'see' anything but the ball dribbling away to the left. The better a putter you become, the easier, of course, it is to imagine the right stroke and to think of the ball doing what you want. When I had problems with my putting I sometimes found it difficult to keep my thoughts positive; I couldn't help but imagine the putt missing. I know from my own experience that I have missed more 3-foot putts because of negative thoughts than because of anything else, such as errors in the stroke or in the way I read the green.

I believe that many people who are bad short-putters in particular could improve their chances of success by spending time simply thinking about making a good stroke and running the ball accurately into the centre of the hole. If you spend just a few minutes each day visualizing a straight putt of perhaps 3 feet and the ball running firmly into the centre of the hole, then this should help you take the right picture out onto the course with you. Hopefully by practising this you will find you can stand over a putt and have a far more positive approach, visualizing success and never failure.

Concentration and Routine

Many golfers find themselves thinking negatively on the course because their concentration lapses and their thinking is not very systematic. If you allow yourself to approach a putt without any set routine or purpose it is awfully easy to become side-tracked. **It is absolutely essential to adopt a set routine for every putt, and to stick to that routine regardless of the score, regardless of the importance of the tournament, and regardless also of the difficulty of the putt.** There are several reasons why I believe a routine is so important. For one thing, a lot of players find it hard to relax between shots yet to be able to concentrate at the right moment. Part of your routine should be on how and when to pinpoint concentration. You may, for example, be quite relaxed chatting to your fellow golfers as you walk to the green and then find it hard to switch off from the conversation. Perhaps your point of concentration should be the moment when you mark the ball, clean it and then replace it, from then on thinking only about your putt and forgetting everything else.

But a routine is also important in making sure that you produce good, accurate judgements. You need to read the green, judge the line and trust your decision. What happens with players who do not adopt a routine is that their level of concentration, and hence their ability to putt well, varies according to the situation. Many golfers will putt pretty well on a putting green when they are taking things casually and not trying particularly hard. They then go on the golf course in a friendly game and also putt quite well. But when they have to play an important putt on the last hole of a match or in a tournament their whole method breaks down. Usually what happens is that they start trying harder the more important they see the occasion, and as they try harder their ability to judge and make decisions alters and in fact gets worse. The average golfer may have

148

A routine is essential: go through the same process at the same speed with the same number of practice swings and looks at the target, whether in practice, play or the pressure of the closing holes of a tournament

one practice swing and look up once at the hole on the putting green; then on the golf course he might increase these to two practice swings and two looks; but by the time he has to putt for the match on the last hole he will be having three practice swings and looking up six or seven times! If his judgement is best when he looks up twice for ordinary play, then he needs to stick to this on a putt which he feels to be particularly important.

It is worth understanding how we make judgements and decisions. If we go back to our idea of tossing a ball at a target, most of us who are in any sense natural games players can do this quite accurately. We can pick up the ball, look at a target and throw it with remarkable accuracy with one quick look. If we were then to look two or three or four times and try to think the throw out very accurately, the odds are that our judgement would not improve at all. In many cases the brain works better when it acts spontaneously than when the thinking becomes slower. Most sports in which the ball is moving require quick reflexes and instinctive thinking, but in a game like golf, in which the ball is stationary, there is sometimes too much time for thought. It is very easy in a tournament to be faced with an important putt and then to look up a couple of extra times, muddling the thinking rather than improving the decision making. Using a definite routine relaxes you. It also means that your muscles are tuned up in the same way each time; it is as though they begin to know what is expected of them each time. The muscles 'remember' the movements they have carried out so many times in practising that stroke with the same routine. This muscle memory is important. Change your routine, and the muscles have less chance to remember the movements which should follow.

A lot of players, both amateurs and professionals, play worse as soon as they are in a tournament situation facing any pressure. Their immediate reaction I think is that they assume that their concentration breaks down and possibly that they are rushing their shots. Often it is just the reverse: by trying too hard they slow down, take longer to think out their shots, put themselves under pressure, and then fail to judge the shots as accurately as they would in practice or in a relaxed game. For this reason Willi Hofmann always encouraged me to use a really definite routine in practice and play, reading the greens in an identical way for each putt, having a precise number of practice swings and looking up at the target a definite number of times. I am fairly slow and deliberate in my routine, but I play like this all the time. Some top professionals are quick, others are slow, but the important point is that most of us prepare for every putt with a rigid, individual routine. Obviously you have to discover what suits you best and adopt your own pattern of play. Try to get used to reading putts in

150

the same way, either from one, two or three directions, depending on how seriously you take the game, and then have a set number of practice swings and looks at the target. Avoid at all costs the temptation to look up just one or two times more on a putt to save the match than you would in practice or on the first green.

Motivation and Trying Too Hard

I suppose the most common complaint from any amateur golfer is that he produces his bad shot just when he wants to produce his best. This obviously happens not just with putting but with the long shots too. Again, it goes back to developing a routine and doing the same thing over and over again. Any successful professional golfer is nearly always something of a perfectionist. I hate producing a bad shot, whether I am on the practice ground or on the golf course. Obviously it is more important if that bad shot is in the closing holes of a major tournament. But the only way I can train myself to perform under pressure is to make nearly all my golf shots extremely important. You frequently see players standing on the driving range hitting balls well but fairly carelessly. Put them on the golf course, and they do not look the same at all. Instead of a relaxed attitude, they now show a degree of pressure by wanting to succeed. Put that same player in a situation in which he faces a really difficult shot or has a crucial putt in a competition, and his whole mental approach and preparation for the shot alters. Obviously I cannot say that I am motivated in exactly the same way to hit a shot on the practice ground as I am in a tournament, but the desire for perfection is pretty constant for all my shots. Over and over again I spent hours on the putting green hitting a little putt and telling myself it was a putt for the Open or the Masters. I have rehearsed these putts time and again with real desire to hole them. **A lot of golfers ruin their chances of doing well in competitions because they are used to playing many of their shots or hitting many of their putts quite casually without real desire; then, in a competition, they try too hard – harder than they can cope with – and change their routine**. Tension creeps in because they are not used to the pressure. You have to figure out what level of motivation suits you best and then try to work at that level the whole time. Perhaps you should modify your attitude in practice and friendly games so that you become more highly motivated and more of a perfectionist; or perhaps you should train yourself to play in a competition with a very relaxed attitude, convincing yourself that it doesn't really matter. One approach suits some people, but not others. You

Seve in action. A player with tremendous motivation, concentration and great pride of performance should approach putts in a systematic way regardless of the score. I sometimes hear amateur golfers telling their caddies how important a putt is because it is for a birdie or a par. In reality every putt is just as important and when you add the score up at the end of the day a putt missed on the 1st or 2nd counts just as much as one missed on the 18th. You also have to motivate yourself just the same whether you are 5 under par or 5 over par. Some players tend to get very nervous if they are doing well, whereas others get nervous or concerned if doing badly. As far as possible most players need to shut out any thoughts of their total score and concentrate on each putt, with the idea of playing it as well as possible. After all, if you are faced with a putt of 8 feet on a particular hole, it is exactly the same task facing you whether it is for a par or a birdie, whether you are doing well or badly. But often players lose concentration or try too hard, change their routine and produce their worst instead of their best.

Many players put themselves under unnecessary pressure. Obviously for a professional like myself, holing a putt to win the Masters Championship, or to win any tournament for that matter, is immensely important. It can change your life and give your family security. For professional golfers there are a few putts that can change their whole career. But for almost all players a missed putt or a lost competition is often seen out of all proportion. Players put themselves under quite unwarranted and unnecessary pressure, when in reality the result is probably forgotten a matter of hours, days or at the most weeks later. I believe that the player who suffers from tournament pressure really does need to see things in perspective.

When I play golf I like to feel relaxed. I know that problems arose in my putting when I used to become tense. Again, this is a question of motivating yourself at a pretty constant level so that you do not suffer from trying too hard at an important moment. If you adopt a routine it helps you stay relaxed because you walk onto every green knowing precisely how you are going to approach the putt. Without a routine you can easily start worrying about your actual approach to the shot. There are two aspects to relaxation, the first being mental and the second physical. **To me mental relaxation is a matter of trying to stay calm, of knowing the routine and stroke I am going to use, and of being able to treat each putt as a separate little task without worrying about what has gone before or what is to come in the round.** Physical relaxation in my putting is important, particularly having the feeling of keeping my arms and wrists relaxed and my grip fairly loose. A lot of professionals have very definite ways of relaxing under the pressure of a tournament. Some

Adopting a rigid routine gives me a certain security in times of pressure. I walk onto the green knowing precisely the task and putting plan ahead of me. With this repetitive approach I am unlikely to be sidetracked into worrying how I will tackle the putt. My energies can all go on sound reading of the green, feeling the texture of the ground beneath my feet, looking for any little clues as to speed and slope, and at the same time taking a few deep breaths to compose myself if necessary

achieve this by walking onto the green and taking a few very deep breaths; others let their arms and hands hang loosely as if trying to feel any tension dripping out of the ends of the fingers.

Keeping a good rhythm is also important, not just for the long game but also for the short game and putting. Adopting the kind of routine I have explained above can help keep the rhythm for the stroke. Some players find it hard to keep a rhythm and tend to slow down or speed up their approach, losing the timing of the stroke in the process. Many tournament players work very hard at an overall timing for the full round of golf, walking at a consistent speed, taking just the same amount of time preparing for every shot, in reading the greens and lining up every putt.

154

The moment of decision.
It must be positive and
precise. I look worried by
this one!

Strategy and Scoring

Two of the most important points on any putt are that your decision
making is positive and that you have a good picture of what you are trying
to produce. There should be a definite aim and object for every putt, not
just in the direction but also in the speed. Never putt while you are in any
doubt about the line or the speed. Be positive. A wrong decision is generally
less disastrous than being indecisive and making no real decision at all.
As I explained earlier, the right way of approaching most putts is to ensure
that the ball will run about 15 inches past the hole if it misses. This means
that the putt back should be little problem but that the ball will reach the

hole travelling with sufficient speed to hold its line. There is, however, a definite approach needed for certain putts which may vary according to the way you are scoring. If I were faced with a putt of 10 yards to tie for an Open Championship, there is no way I would want to leave the putt a few inches short or even contemplate lagging it up close. There would be little point in being conservative. Having a go to force a tie for a play-off would be far more important than ensuring second place instead of third. I would therefore approach the putt pretty boldly. With two putts to win the championship I would obviously play the putt with a different idea in mind, now making quite certain of lagging the putt within 12 inches or so to leave myself a simple tap in. Similarly in matchplay if I had a putt for a half I would attack the hole quite aggressively, being able to play the putt with little borrow and without worrying about charging past.

In strokeplay I believe that the correct strategy for most golfers is to think of running a long putt 12–15 inches past the hole, giving yourself a chance of a single putt but looking for safety in the return. Many players constantly try to lag the ball up close to the hole, working only at 2-putting, and then end up 3-putting because their approach putt is unsatisfactorily short. For the serious student of golf I would suggest you

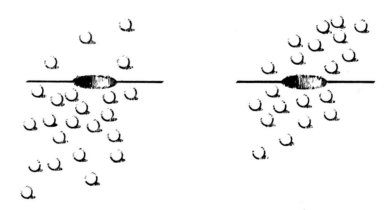

It is worth thinking carefully about the length of medium and long putts which fail. Most players plotting their failures would probably find a pattern of results rather like the left-hand drawing, the balls tending to fall short. A good long-putter might find roughly equal numbers of putts short and past like the right-hand one. The exceptionally good putter would probably hope for almost every putt to pass the hole with the results centred round a spot a few inches beyond it. The drawings indicate results of individual putts rather than a group of balls present simultaneously

156

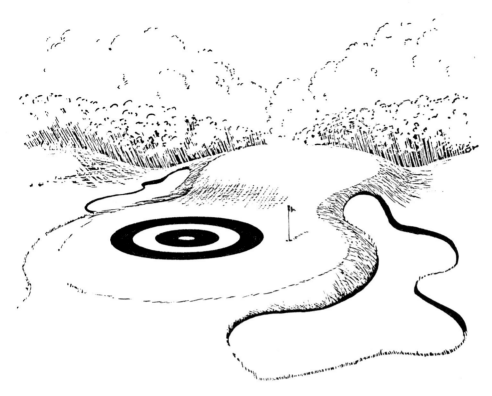

Putting can be made much easier with good iron shots. In this example good sense dictates that the shot should be aimed to the heart of the green and well clear of the bunker. It also suggests leaving the shot short of the flag for an uphill putt, rather than a tricky one down and across the slope

analyse your putting quite critically over a month or a whole golfing season to assess your long-putting performance. Keep a note of the approximate length of each putt, whether uphill or downhill, and the approximate length if you run short or past. This can be filled in very simply in shorthand form on a card and will show where the errors occur. Many players will find that their long putts very rarely pass the hole, and that their 3-putting almost always occurs from a cautious first putt. If your overall putting distance is fairly well judged, you should find roughly equal numbers of long, lay-up putts going short and going past, with the distances short and past more or less balancing. The exceptionally good long-putter would hope for almost every putt to pass the hole and for the results to centre on a spot just past the hole. For medium-length putts, in which you hope for a single putt, you would certainly want the results centred on a point a few inches past the hole to show a more aggressive approach. It is not always easy to see where your own faults lie unless you make some kind of accurate survey in this way to pinpoint the errors. Obviously there are some occasions when you very definitely want to leave the ball short or past, perhaps to leave yourself an uphill return rather than a downhill one, but, as a rough guide, there should always be this feeling of wanting every ball to reach or pass the hole.

Setting yourself up to putt well stems right from the shot you play into the green. Most professional golfers will play what we call the percentage shot, in other words, a shot which allows for a little error but without in any way being negative in our thinking. In other words, if the flag is tucked away in the corner of the green behind a sand trap, I am unlikely to play directly at the flag if an error of 5–6 feet could see my ball drop short in the trap or roll away off the side of the green. I would see this as a dangerous shot and look for a safer area on the green which would avoid pitfalls but still leave me safely placed for my birdie putt. It isn't a question of being cautious or negative but of simply allowing for the inevitable errors of a less than absolutely perfect shot. On a course like Augusta where the greens are particularly sloping, part of the strategy of playing onto the greens has to take into account the difficulty of the birdie putt. On some greens it can be a disaster to roll 10–12 feet past the flag, leaving a pretty impossible putt, whereas being anything up to 25 feet short of the flag can give a relatively straightforward uphill putt. The contour of the green may well indicate whether I want to be to the right or to the left of the flag, not just from the point of view of safety but to leave the easiest putt possible. Obviously professional golfers have a lot more control over their iron shots and can think in this way, whereas many amateur golfers probably find it hard to aim at the green other than directly at the flag. Certainly once you are faced with a short chip, a pitch or a long approach putt you may find that the contours of a very sloping green definitely favour erring to one side of the hole or the other.

Where strategy can be most important is in matchplay in which you not only find yourself playing the golf course but also have to adjust to your opponent's play throughout the whole round. Major strokeplay tournaments become the same sort of challenge in the last few holes when you know precisely your fellow competitors' score and their game can begin